# The Fighting Parson
## of the
# American Revolution

A Biography of
GENERAL PETER MUHLENBERG

Edward W. Hocker

an imprint of Sunbury Press, Inc.
Mechanicsburg, PA  USA

ISBN: 978-1-62006-298-2 (Trade Paperback)

Library of Congress Control Number: 2019955802

FIRST DISTELFINK PRESS EDITION: December 2019


0 1 1 2 3 5 8 13 21 34 55

Set in Adobe Garamond
Designed by Crystal Devine
Cover by Lawrence Knorr
Edited by Lawrence Knorr

*Continue the Enlightenment!*


Cover image: Portrait of Major General Peter Muhlenberg

# CONTENTS

# I

## CHECKERED YOUTH

### Family of Henry Melchior Muhlenberg

There was a time when Americans insisted that their national heroes must make a good showing alongside the heroes of mythology and folklore. To meet the popular taste fact and fable were mingled in the stories of the men who helped to found the United States.

Then came the "debunking" period, when the process of separating myths from history was sometimes carried to the extreme of manufacturing new myths. A great question mark obscured most of the picturesque incidents of the American Revolution as they had long been depicted in literature. In the endeavor to "humanize" the leaders in the revolt against Great Britain, their human failings were sometimes so magnified as to strip these men of all glory.

Peter Muhlenberg, the "fighting parson," is one character of that Revolutionary-era who has withstood the debunkers. It is true, certain stories about him have been shown to be myths. But their elimination has brought to light a greater nobility of character. He was not a pious swashbuckler. His dramatic farewell to the pulpit when he entered the army has been embellished with various impossible trappings. But substantially, the incident must be accepted as history.

His was a strikingly versatile and adaptable career. He was a clergyman, apparently, in two denominations at the same time. He was a native of Pennsylvania, but he commanded Virginia troops. Then he entered upon a political career of distinction in Pennsylvania, and in an era of intense partisan strife, he completely escaped the vituperation and savage attack to which almost every other man prominent in public affairs was subjected.

Samuel W. Pennypacker, the Pennsylvania historian, used to say that no village of its size in the country had produced so many distinguished persons as had Trappe, now a small borough in Montgomery County, Pennsylvania. From the Muhlenberg family came a large proportion of the distinguished persons to whom Pennypacker alluded.

The first of the family was the father of Peter Muhlenberg, the Reverend Henry Melchior Muhlenberg, a native of Eimbeck, in Hanover, who had come to Pennsylvania in 1742 to organize congregations among the numerous German Lutheran settlers of that province. He lived either in Philadelphia or Trappe and exercised superintendence for many years over virtually all the Lutheran congregations of Pennsylvania, New Jersey, Maryland, and Virginia.

At Trappe, Augustus Church was built under his direction in 1743, and to the people worshipping here, his pastoral supervision was especially directed. The old church of 1743 still stands as an impressive religious landmark of colonial times.

In theology, Muhlenberg accepted the milder pietistic Lutheranism as it was taught at the famous Halle Institutions founded by Augustus Herman Francke—the type of theology that called for the translation of faith into action as opposed to the more dogmatic theology which held that formal acceptance of a creed was all that signified. Thus, naturally, Pastor Muhlenberg was a man of action. And so also were his sons.

But the student of heredity will not accord sole honors for Peter Muhlenberg's inherited traits to his father. His mother also came from a family that bred men of action. She was a daughter of Conrad Weiser, pioneer settler of the Tulpehocken region, in what is now Berks County, Pennsylvania, long a frontier leader and famous in the colonial period as a representative of the provincial government in negotiations with the Indians.

There were church troubles in the Tulpehocken region in 1743, and Pastor Muhlenberg visited the locality to try to adjust them. Weiser had originally been of the Reformed or Calvinistic faith. He and other German settlers of the Tulpehocken country fell under the influence of Conrad Beissel, who had founded a monastic community of Seventh-Day Dunkers at Ephrata. Then the efforts of Count Zinzendorf, the Moravian leader, to effect religious unity among the Pennsylvania sects enlisted Weiser's support. Eventually, however, Weiser became a Lutheran. Being the principal resident of the neighborhood, Muhlenberg visited Weiser when he went to Tulpehocken. In the Weiser home was an organ, one of the few in Pennsylvania at that time. Muhlenberg loved music, and he delighted himself and the Weiser household by playing on the organ. There was a daughter, Anna Mary, then 16 years old. The "Tulpehocken Confusion," as the church troubles due to Zinzendorf's activity were called, was not easy to settle, and Muhlenberg had to make further visits to the region. Evidently, he gave consideration to Anna Mary Weiser as well as to the church troubles, for on April 22, 1745, they were married.

The year of his marriage, Pastor Muhlenberg had a house built near the church at Trappe. Up to that time, he lived mostly in Philadelphia. With his young wife, he now made his home at Trappe.

The name of Trappe had not yet come into general use for the place, but it was applied to a tavern kept by members of the Schrack family. There were only a few houses nearby. The region was called Providence, or sometimes New Providence. Originally this territory had been included in William Penn's Manor of Gilberts. In 1729 Providence Township was created, comprising the present Upper Providence and Lower Providence Townships and the boroughs of Collegeville and Trappe. The main highway from Philadelphia to Reading ran through Trappe, the latter place being twenty-five miles northwest of Philadelphia. In 1741 Providence Township had 146 taxable inhabitants. Thereafter new settlers rapidly took up lands.

At Trappe, there was also a congregation of the German Reformed or Calvinist church which had been organized about the time of

Muhlenberg's arrival and which held its services in the Lutheran church until 1755, when it built its own church.

Just how the name of Trappe originated has been a subject of dispute among historians. Pastor Muhlenberg wrote in 1780 that the Schrack Tavern in early days was partly underground, and a certain English farmer when he came home late explained to his inquisitive wife that he had been caught in the trap at Schrack's. Thus, the tavern became popularly known as "the trap." Francis Rawn Shunk, who was born at Trappe and later became governor of Pennsylvania, declined to accept this explanation. His version was that in front of the Schrack Tavern was a flight of steps. "Treppe" is German for steps. Therefore, the tavern was called "Die Treppe," or "The Steps." The question was debated at a meeting of the community's citizens in 1835 when the majority decided to spell the name "Trapp." Later, however, the present orthography of Trappe was generally accepted. Up to recent times, the definite article was commonly used with the name, the place being called "The Trappe."

Neither of the explanations is altogether convincing. It may be that in some way, the name of the valley of La Trappe, near Mortagne, France, was applied to this locality. There the order of Trappist monks has had its headquarters since the twelfth century. Writers not familiar with Pennsylvania's Trappe have sometimes presented it as the seat of a Trappist monastery whose solemn inhabitants practice perpetual silence and other austerities of this order. The predominance of religious influences in the early history of Trappe may have been conducive to the confusion with the French La Trappe.

Here in Trappe, the first son of Pastor Muhlenberg was born, October 1, 1746 (old style). At his baptism, on October 14, he was named John Peter Gabriel Muhlenberg. The sponsors at the baptism were the Reverend Peter Brunnholtz, then pastor of the Lutheran churches of Philadelphia and Germantown; the Reverend Gabriel Naesmann, pastor of the Swedish Lutheran Church at Wicaco, in the southern part of Philadelphia County; John Nicholas Kurtz, then a schoolmaster of the Lutheran congregation at New Hanover and later ordained to the ministry; and John Frederick Vigera, schoolmaster of the Philadelphia Lutheran congregation.

It was the custom among the Germans of those times to bestow the name of John upon most boys and the name of Mary upon most girls, along with one or more additional given names. As the children grew to maturity, they often abandoned the John or Mary. The oldest son of the Trappe pastor abandoned both John and Gabriel and wrote his name simply Peter Muhlenberg, or preferably even shorter, "P. Muhlenberg."

## Pennsylvania in Muhlenberg's Youth

Those were times of uncertainty and fear in interior Pennsylvania. England, the mother country, had gone to war with France in 1744, in the conflict known as King George's War. Pennsylvania, along with the other American dependencies of England, was expected to supply troops to attack the French in Canada. But the Quakers controlled the Pennsylvania Assembly, and, being opposed to warfare, they refused to vote appropriations for military purposes. While William Penn had been a Quaker, the Penns of this era, who were the proprietaries of Pennsylvania, no longer adhered to Quakerism but were attached to the Church of England. For many years, until the Quakers lost control of the Assembly, the question of voting appropriations to the proprietaries for purposes concerned with war was a source of controversy.

Curiously enough, a large proportion of the German settlers, though not Quakers and not holding to a pacifist faith, supported the Quaker candidates for Assembly and thus helped them maintain power, which they could not have done with their own strength. The Germans took no great interest in political disputes and did not often have candidates of their own stock. The German newspaper, which Christopher Sauer published in Germantown, circulated widely among German settlers. This newspaper supported the Quaker policy, Sauer, though not attached to any religious group, being an adherent of pacifism. A phase of the matter that appealed to the Germans with greater power than the abstract theories of opposition to warfare was the economic issue involved. Thrift was their outstanding trait. They objected to the waste of money, either for personal purposes or for the government. The spending of money on armies looked to them like waste, and it was sure to increase taxes. Hence, when they took the trouble to vote at all, they were likely to vote with the Quakers, with the hope that if the Quakers remained in power, taxes would not be increased. The Quakers and Germans constituted what was known as the Country Party, while the opposition was the Gentlemen's or City Party.

But Conrad Weiser also wielded great influence among the German settlers, and this influence was exerted to the full degree on behalf of the proprietaries and against the dominant Quakers. Pastor Muhlenberg had little to say about civic and military controversies, but naturally, he must have sympathized with the appeals of Weiser for aid in defending the frontier against Indian ravages. Most of the tribes took the side of the French whenever France and England made war in America. The natives seized the opportunity to attack exposed settlements, and the pleas of the people for help from the provincial authorities in Philadelphia were in vain. But at last, the equanimity of the Philadelphia Quakers also was disturbed when French and Spanish privateers attacked towns along the Atlantic Coast as close as New Castle, Delaware. Then the Pennsylvania Assembly was induced to vote £4000 for the King's use, "in the purchase of bread, beef, pork, flour, wheat, and other grain." Benjamin Franklin and other opponents of the pacifist policy interpreted "other grain" to include grains of gunpowder, and some of the money was thus expended. Franklin also organized bodies of volunteer troops, enrolling 10,000 men throughout the province.

Peace terminated King George's War in 1748. But within six years, England and France were again at war, and a fine British army, under General Braddock, met disastrous defeat in Western Pennsylvania in 1755. Again natives, co-operating with the French, attacked frontier settlers. Conrad Weiser and a force of volunteers from Berks County marched to the defense of the people of the Susquehanna region in 1755, but they could find no hostile Indians. Weiser was busy trying to devise protective measures, but his efforts to obtain help from the Assembly failed, and finally, in exasperation, he threatened to lead the Berks County Germans into Philadelphia to present their protests and demands in person. However, the threat was not put into execution.

All through his boyhood, Peter Muhlenberg undoubtedly heard stories of warfare and conflict engendered by those times. Weiser visited the Muhlenberg family on his trips to and from Philadelphia, and it is likely the boy was thrilled by his grandfather's recital of affairs, a recital in which avoidance of military service had no part. Thus, it may readily be understood how the son of the Trappe parsonage developed a liking for army activities.

There were periods when Pastor Muhlenberg, the father, was away from home for long intervals, engaged in church work in distant settlements. At one time, about 1755, when both Muhlenberg and his wife seem to have been absent. Peter and his sister, Eve Elizabeth, were placed in the care of an English woman living in New Hanover, a well-educated woman who had no children of her own. New Hanover, where there was a Lutheran congregation even older than that at Trappe, was nine miles northwest of the latter place. Through this experience, Peter Muhlenberg received valuable training in the English language. German was commonly spoken at home, though the father was conversant with English and occasionally preached in that language.

Some Lutheran congregations on the Raritan River in northern New Jersey claimed Pastor Muhlenberg's oversight during the 1750s when they were without a pastor. They wanted him to assume the active pastorate among them. He made long visits there in 1757 and 1758, and the following year he, his wife, and four of the children were in the Raritan region during the spring and summer. At this time, the Muhlenberg home in Trappe, where three children remained, no doubt the older ones, was in the charge of William Graaf, a schoolmaster whom Muhlenberg was preparing for the ministry. In November, Graaf and his wife, taking Peter Muhlenberg with them, traveled to the Raritan region, where they spent three weeks. In December, Mrs. Muhlenberg and two of the children returned to Trappe with the Graafs, Peter, and two of the other children remaining with their father.

About this time, Pastor Muhlenberg wrote thus in his diary about Peter: "He does not care much about female society, but is bent on hunting and fishing."

Evidently, Peter was enjoying himself thoroughly in his own way as a normal boy would, for boys of thirteen, if they are normal, are much more interested in hunting and fishing than in female society. Yet, as will develop later, Peter's propensity for outdoor sports caused his father much concern.

In January 1760, Peter returned to Trappe with his father. Eight years later, Peter Muhlenberg was to go again to the Raritan region, this time as a minister of the gospel.

## Sent Abroad to be Educated

In 1761, the Muhlenberg family removed from Trappe to Philadelphia. The rapidly growing Lutheran congregation in that city had all along been nominally under Pastor Muhlenberg's supervision. Now he took active charge of that flock.

No doubt he was actuated in some degree to make this change to provide better educational opportunities for his children, of whom there were now six living, while two had died. Three more children were born in Philadelphia. Peter, with two younger brothers, Frederick Augustus Conrad, born in 1750, and Gotthilf Henry, born in 1753, went to school in the Academy department of the College of Philadelphia, which later developed into the University of Pennsylvania. The institution, then situated on Fourth Street, below Arch, was under the management of the Reverend Dr. William Smith, a clergyman of the Church of England, with whom the father of the three Muhlenberg boys had become intimate some years before when the English Society for the Propagation of Christian Knowledge was endeavoring to establish free schools in the German settlements of Pennsylvania. Pastor Muhlenberg supported the movement and opened schools under the auspices of the society in several of his congregations. Nevertheless, most of the Germans were suspicious of the undertaking, fearing it was an insidious attack upon their language and religion, and Sauer's German newspaper left nothing undone to foster this suspicion. The schools were continued only a few years. Among the trustees of the society were Dr. Smith, Benjamin Franklin, and Conrad Weiser.

The University of Pennsylvania has included General Muhlenberg among its "eminent sons" of the eighteenth century whose memory is recalled by tablets on the walls of Houston Club, at the University. His connection with the institution is there described thus: "College, 1763."

Although Dr. Smith's Philadelphia school was legally empowered to confer college degrees, Pastor Muhlenberg wanted his sons to have the benefit of training in one of the long-established schools of Germany. The second year of the family's stay in Philadelphia, he corresponded with the Reverend Dr. Jacob Duche, one of the assistant ministers of the Anglican congregation worshiping at Christ Church, Philadelphia, about a contemplated trip abroad by that clergyman and the possibility of his taking Peter Muhlenberg along with him, but the project was not consummated. But in the spring of 1763, the father arranged to have his three sons go to England with William Allen, chief justice of the province, who had also been one of the trustees of the ineffective free school movement. Chief Justice Allen was reputed to be the richest man in Pennsylvania at that time.

On April 27, 1763, Peter, then in his 17th year; Frederick, aged 13; and Henry, aged 10, set sail with Chief Justice Allen, embarking at Philadelphia on the ship of Captain Budden. Ceremonious solemnity marked the farewell in the Muhlenberg home. The father offered prayer, and the Reverend Charles Magnus Wrangel, provost of the Swedish churches along the Delaware River, addressed the departing youths and their family and then pronounced the benediction. For some reason not evident, the father did not accompany the boys to the ship. But the mother did and remained until the vessel put out from the wharf at 4 o'clock.

Onboard the ship, the Muhlenberg boys found two friends of the family—Henry Keppele, Jr., a son of one of the officials of the Philadelphia

Lutheran church, and Justus Frederick Meyer. For just seven weeks, the travelers were on the ship, arriving in London on June 15. The Muhlenberg boys had letters from their father to the Reverend Frederick Michael Ziegenhagen, Lutheran court preacher in London, who had assisted the father on his journey to America twenty-one years before and had given aid from time to time to Lutheran congregations in Pennsylvania. They also had a letter from Provost Wrangel to a firm of merchants in London. The recipients of the letters arranged to have the boys continue their travels by way of Hamburg and Eimbeck to Halle, where the father had planned that his three sons were to be enrolled as students in the famous Lutheran institutions. Here the father had been a teacher in his youth.

These institutions were the source of the missionary endeavors which had brought the elder Muhlenberg to America. Augustus Herman Francke, a Lutheran clergyman prominent in the pietistic revolt against sterile theological dogma, had founded the Halle Institutions, beginning with an orphanage and gradually expanding until various schools and a missionary department were included along with a publishing house and a medical branch. Bibles and other religious books used among the Germans in Pennsylvania came largely from Halle, as did the remedies with which they contended against sickness. In Halle, there was also a famous university, which should not be confounded with the Francke Institutions.

## The Myth of His Wild Youth

This stay in Halle is associated with the earliest Peter Muhlenberg myth—the story that he got into a fight with a teacher, ran away from the school, and joined the German army. Based upon this myth, there was built the legend of a wild, harum-scarum youth developing into a blustering maturity.

Some strictures contained in letters written by an unduly exacting father helped to give credence to the unwarranted tales. The truth of the matter seems to be that Pastor Muhlenberg became alarmed because his first-born son showed tendencies of being a real boy. In a letter to Dr.

Ziegenhagen, October 27, 1763, discussing the sending of the boys to Germany, he wrote:

> My son Peter has, alas! enjoyed but little of my care and control, on account of my extensive official duties, but he has had no evil example from his parents and many reproofs and counsels. His chief fault and bad inclination have been his fondness for hunting and fishing. But if our most revered fathers at Halle observe any tendency to vice, I would humbly beg that they send him to a well-disciplined garrison town, under the name of Peter Weiser, before he causes much trouble or complaint. There he may obey the drum if he will not follow the spirit of God. My prayers will follow him, and if his soul only is saved, be he in what condition he may, I shall be content. I well know what Satan wishes for me and mine.

The chief fault thus set forth—his fondness for hunting and fishing—certainly is not sufficient to convict the boy of possessing vicious tendencies, and the suggestion about disciplining him savors of brutality in the light of modern understanding. But that was an age when brutality was often deemed essential in the rearing of boys.

Not until the Reverend Dr. William Germann made an exhaustive examination of records and correspondence covering Peter Muhlenberg's stay in Germany at that time was the unreliability of the long-accepted tradition proven. What Dr. Germann found indicated clearly that as a lad, Peter Muhlenberg had been a victim of monstrous injustice and that his own kin and admirers had been libeling his memory for generations by fostering the intimation that he was guilty of dishonorable acts.

Peter Muhlenberg never became a student in the Halle schools nor in any other school in Germany. Frederick and Henry were enrolled in the Halle Institutions. But the documents found at Halle show that Peter was shipped off to Lubeck, near Hamburg, and apprenticed to a storekeeper there. The original articles of apprenticeship were discovered, showing that Peter Muhlenberg, son of the great Lutheran leader in America, was bound out for six years in the care of a man who was nothing more than a small grocer and liquor dealer.

The subsequent correspondence makes it clear that the Reverend Gotthilf August Francke, son of the founder of the institutions and then at their head, knew nothing about the man with whom he was placing Peter; that the merchant in Lubeck had asked the orphanage officials in Halle to send him one of the orphans as an apprentice, and they delivered Peter Muhlenberg into his hands. In the subsequent attempts to explain the matter, Dr. Francke said, and Peter admitted, that the boy wanted to learn a business. It was supposed he was to have an opportunity to become a druggist. But the only drugs he was permitted to handle consisted of alcoholic drinks.

The articles of apprenticeship show that during those six years, the master was to give the boy only his food and lodging. Dr. Francke was to provide his clothing. If the lad served honorably and faithfully for six years, he was to receive at the end of the term a black suit of clothes, a hat, cane, shoes, and stockings, or, instead of this, 100 marks in money.

If Peter Muhlenberg was a wild, reckless daredevil, it is difficult to imagine his enduring such outrageously severe discipline. He signed the papers because he thought he was going to learn the drug business in a large establishment. The place turned out to be a little shop where he was the only employee. There was a small drug department, but Peter was not admitted to it. All he did was measure out groceries and liquor over the counter. He worked every day, including Sunday, and every night until 10 o'clock.

For two full years, he clung to this distasteful job before making complaints. Then in the meekest manner possible, he mentioned in a letter to his father that he suffered from cold in the winter and from lack of proper clothing, that he had to wear the same shirt four weeks continuously and that he was learning nothing. The "business" in which he was supposed to be gaining proficiency, he said, was of a kind that anyone might learn in four weeks. He added that apprenticeship terms in occupations where there was something to learn were usually of four years duration, whereas his was six.

Dr. Muhlenberg began a circumspect investigation that lasted some months. He sought the aid of Dr. Ziegenhagen, in London, who wrote to Dr. Francke, in Halle. Dr. Francke, at first was disposed to ignore the matter. But finally, an official of the Halle Institutions made inquiries in Lubeck and learned that the boy had minimized rather than exaggerated the situation.

Then at the behest of Dr. Muhlenberg, efforts were begun to have the boy freed. The employer demanded the payment of 100 thalers (about $75) for cutting off two years from the six-year term of apprenticeship. An agreement was made for the release of Peter at Easter 1767, upon payment of the sum demanded. This agreement was signed in August 1766. A few days later, young Peter was missing.

It transpired that he had joined a regiment of troops in Lubeck—not a German regiment, as most accounts say—but an English regiment that was being recruited. Lubeck was a "free city," and Great Britain at that time had the right to recruit troops there. Moreover, it was not a regiment of dragoons, as the old stories aver, but the Sixtieth Regiment of Foot.

In this phase of Peter Muhlenberg's adventures, little was available except sources inimical to him. But reading between the lines of the letters that have been preserved, there was a captain in this regiment with whom Peter Muhlenberg became friendly. Perhaps the captain made the acquaintance of the lad in the store and found he was a bright young fellow. Naturally, they would be drawn together because both spoke English. Then homesickness welled up in the lad's heart. This regiment was being recruited to go to America. Why should he not join it and go home—cut loose from this abominable grocery and liquor shop, join the regiment, and sail for America?

When the employer came storming around the recruiting office, the captain told him the boy was now in the British army and would remain there unless he himself chose to go back to the shop. The boy did not hesitate about deciding, and the shopkeeper went home without his apprentice.

Through the friendly captain, Peter Muhlenberg was at once made secretary of the regiment—a position much more compatible with the youth's talents than that of standing behind the counter in a small store.

After a few months, the regiment arrived in America, and here it was quickly arranged that Muhlenberg should be released from military service upon payment of a small sum that had been expended for his clothing.

Evidently, Father Muhlenberg saw things in a clearer light later, for after Peter had come home, the father wrote regarding the payment he had to make to the son's former employer: "It is certainly a dear ransom for two years and a half. If I had put the boy in a grocery and liquor shop here, he would have received his board and clothing for four years and wages beside."

Henry Melchior Muhlenberg, father of
Peter Muhlenberg

Gotthilf Muhlenberg, brother of
Peter Muhlenberg

Augustus Church in Trappe, Pennsylvania

AVGVSTVS HERMANNVS FRANCKIVS,
S. THEOL. PROFESS. ORDIN. IN ACADEM. HALENSI,
IBIDEM AD D. VLR. PASTOR ET GYMNASII SCHOLARCHA,
ITEMQ. PAEDAGOGII REGII ET ORPHANOTROPHEI GLAVCHE
DIRECTOR I.
NATVS LVBECAE A. MDCLXIII. D. .... MARE DENAT. HAL AE. DVIII. IVN. MDCCXVI

Augustus Herman Francke

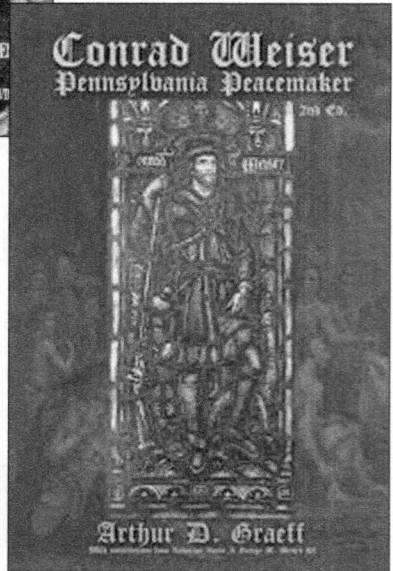

Conrad Weiser: Pennsylvania
Peacemaker by Arthur Graeff has
many details about the grandfather
of Peter Muhlenberg

Ephrata Cloister

Count Zinzendorf

Conrad Weiser's home near Womelsdorf, Pennsylvania

Henry Melchior Muhlenberg's first house in Trappe, Pennsylvania

Francis Rawn Shunk

Benjamin Franklin

Justice William Allen

Reverend Dr. William Smith

Reverend Frederick Michael Ziegenhagen

## II

# IN THE MINISTRY

## A Popular Preacher

Notwithstanding the son preferred a business life, the father was determined he should follow in his own footsteps, as a dutiful elder son
should, and thus, now that the boy was home again, steps were taken to
have him educated for the ministry in the best method then possible in
Pennsylvania. There were no theological seminaries in the province in
those years. Youths who wished to become clergymen took a course of
instruction with some established minister. The elder Muhlenberg was
still serving the big Philadelphia Lutheran parish, which probably left
him little time to instruct his son. Or perhaps it may have dawned upon
him by this time that someone other than himself might be better able to
understand Peter. At any rate, Peter became a student under the provost
of the Swedish Lutheran churches on the Delaware River, the Reverend
Dr. Charles Magnus Wrangel. Dr. Wrangel's influence seems to have
been beneficial, and if the boy at first was hostile toward thoughts of
becoming a pastor, Dr. Wrangel brought him to an appreciation of the
office for which he was to be trained.

Already in the early months of 1768, when Dr. Wrangel was absent,
Peter Muhlenberg sometimes preached for him in Gloria Dei Church,
which still stands, near Christian and Swanson Streets, along the Delaware River, in the lower part of Philadelphia. His efforts pleased the

people, and the vestry requested him to serve further as a substitute when occasion required.

It became noticeable that when he was announced to preach at Gloria Dei Church, there was a diminished attendance and collection at Saint Michael's German Lutheran Church, in Philadelphia, many of the Germans going to the Swedish church to hear the son of their pastor. Some of the people of Saint Michael's Church suggested that Peter Muhlenberg be permitted to preach in their church. To this, the father consented, and Peter took charge of the service in that church, on Fifth Street, above Arch, on the evening of Good Friday, 1768. The theme of his sermon was "The Burial of Christ." The father was not present at this service. Afterward, he wrote this about it:

> There was such a concourse and throng in Saint Michael's as never before had taken place, as they told me, since the church was erected, I did not go there, but stayed at home in my small chamber, feeling like a condemned publican and a worm, with tears praying the Chief Shepherd and Bishop of souls to defend this act against Satan's cunning and to grant that the good cause might not suffer through me or mine. After service, the elders came to my house and congratulated me with much feeling on the sermon delivered by my son. I thanked them, but no one knoweth what is the state of my mind in anything of this sort, since I am slow to believe or trust in any good, either in myself or in my own, save what God's grace and mercy give. I could not take it ill in my brethren in Christ that they secretly, out of love to the cause, said to each other, "God be praised! If the old man should depart, Providence has sent us a young substitute who, in case of need, may assist and comfort us."

Thereafter, Peter Muhlenberg was regularly employed as an assistant to his father, supplying pulpits throughout southeastern Pennsylvania, especially in struggling congregations, which found it difficult to maintain a pastor. Among the places where he preached were Barren Hill, in what is now Montgomery County; Pikeland, in Chester County; and Macungie, now Lehigh County. All this time, his father never heard him preach, but he would criticize the manuscripts of his son's sermons.

The Macungie congregation considered calling Peter Muhlenberg as a pastor, and it was also proposed that he serve as a missionary among the natives. Some Christianized Indians living near the borders of Pennsylvania and New York had made an appeal for ministers and teachers, and the Reverend Richard Peters, Anglican minister in Philadelphia, suggested that Peter Muhlenberg and Christian Streit, both German Lutheran candidates for the ministry and both students under Dr. Wrangel, be asked to assume this work.

But the development of events brought it about that Peter Muhlenberg's first pastorate was that of several Lutheran congregations near the Raritan River in northern New Jersey.

## Pastor in New Jersey

It has sometimes been asserted that the Reverend Henry Melchior Muhlenberg, about this time, ordained his son to the ministry. Of such action, no record exists, and it is not likely that Peter Muhlenberg ever received Lutheran ordination. It was not unusual in those times for young candidates for the ministry to serve many years of apprenticeship. The Ministerium of Pennsylvania would license such candidates to preach, but ordination was delayed.

At the session of the Ministerium in Philadelphia in 1769, when Peter Muhlenberg was present, representing the congregations of northern New Jersey, a committee was appointed to examine him and another candidate. The outcome, so far as the archives of the Ministerium show, was nothing further than the issuing of a license to him to serve as assistant to his father in the New Jersey congregations.

For these new duties, Peter Muhlenberg made his home in New Germantown, in the northeastern part of what is now Hunterdon County. With this region, he was not unfamiliar, for, as has been told, he spent some time hereabouts when his father was ministering to the Lutherans of the region in 1759.

The first settlers here, about 1700, had been English, and the village was first called Smithfield, for Ralph Smith, leader of the community. As the century advanced, numerous German and Dutch settlers came, and in time they outnumbered the English element so that in 1749, Ralph Smith sold the church in the village to the German Lutherans. The elder Muhlenberg had kept a watchful eye over the congregations along the Raritan. About 1760, the Lutherans built a church at Bedminstertown, also called Pluckamin, in the northern part of the present Somerset County, adjoining Hunterdon County on the east.

Records of the two congregations begin in 1767, when, through the instrumentality of the Reverend Henry Melchior Muhlenberg, a charter was obtained from the provincial authorities for the congregations under the title of "the rector, churchwardens, and vestrymen of the United Zion and Saint Paul's Churches and congregations in the counties of Hunterdon, Somerset, and Morris." The title was according to the usage of the Church of England, not that of the Lutherans. The Reverend Henry Melchior Muhlenberg was recognized as rector, though still a pastor in Philadelphia. His son, as assistant pastor, assumed active charge, somewhat like the English vicar. In the church records, he is denominated the "pro tem rector." He entered upon his duties early in 1769.

The older congregation, in New Germantown, adopted the name Zion, and that in Bedminstertown Saint Paul's. The charge also included Saint James' Church, Greenwich Township, now Warren County. In 1770 the vestry resolved that "the pro tem rector or his regular assistant minister" should hold services every second Sunday and feast day in Zion Church, should have possession of the glebe, should preach every fourth Sunday in Roxbury, called the Valley, and receive from that congregation £20, and should also receive £20 for preaching and catechizing children in Bedminstertown.

The fact that Peter Muhlenberg never was the actual rector or pastor of these New Jersey congregations probably explains why he was not ordained. According to Lutheran usage, a candidate who has successfully passed an examination in theology is not ordained until he has received and accepted a "call" in due form to become pastor of a congregation. Peter Muhlenberg in New Jersey was always an assistant to his father, the latter being nominally rector.

While Peter Muhlenberg was in Philadelphia in June 1769, attending the meeting of the Lutheran Ministerium of Pennsylvania, when he was examined and licensed to preach, he also took part in the dedication of a new church for his father's congregation in Philadelphia. This church, named Zion, did not supplant old Saint Michael's Church but was needed in addition to the old church to accommodate the large congregation, the largest in the city. Thereafter services were held every Sunday in both churches, though there continued to be but one congregational organization. The chief pastor had the aid of one and sometimes two assistant ministers.

On the morning of Sunday, June 25, 1769, the ministers attending the Ministerium meeting met in Saint Michael's Church, Fifth Street, above Arch, which had been dedicated in 1748. They led a procession comprising congregational officials carrying the communion and baptismal vessels, officials of the German Reformed congregation, and lay delegates attending the Ministerium meeting. Thus, with the church bells ringing, they marched about two blocks to the new church at Fourth and Cherry Streets.

The clergy walked in eight pairs, the youngest first and the elder Dr. Muhlenberg last, accompanied by the Reverend Casper Diedrich Weyberg, the Reformed pastor. Peter Muhlenberg and George Young, both of whom were licensed as assistant ministers at this session, made up the second pair.

Arriving at the new church, the choir, with two French horns, took the lead, and the procession passed into the church, singing the old German choral, "*O heiliger Geist, kehr bey uns ein.* [It was stirring to the senses and impressive to the spirit]," wrote the elder Muhlenberg.

After the procession had entered through the main doorway, four other doors were opened to the people, and soon the building was crowded. The elder Muhlenberg then conducted the consecration. In the ceremony, each of the attending ministers, in the order of seniority, recited a passage from the Scriptures. Peter Muhlenberg, who came twelfth, being a native son of America, paid tribute "to the benefactors of the building of Zion in this country." His Scriptural citation was Psalm 122: 6, 7:

> Pray for the peace of Jerusalem: they shall prosper that love thee.
> Peace be within thy walls, and prosperity within thy palaces.

The elder Muhlenberg then preached the sermon, based upon Isaiah 43: 1-6. He was sick and weak, being much concerned about the details of the service and having sat up until 3 A.M. the previous night, after which he had only three hours' sleep. The vapors from the fresh paint and plaster accentuated his fatigue and illness. Furthermore, as he entered the church, he was told that one of his grandchildren had just died. Thus, he was compelled to curtail the sermon he had written. Upon going home, he took to his bed and could not take part in the afternoon service.

On Monday morning there was a further service in the new church in which the clergy of the English-speaking churches of the city, the faculty of the college, and city officials participated, the Reverend Richard Peters, of the Anglican church, preaching the sermon.

The church building in the dedication of which Peter Muhlenberg thus had a part was 108 feet long and seventy feet wide, and it had the largest auditorium in Philadelphia. Its interior was richly ornamented, and eight pillars supported the roof. Later an organ made by David Tannenberger of Lititz, Pennsylvania, was placed in position and was declared to be the largest and finest organ in America. At the time of the British occupancy of Philadelphia in the Revolution, the church became a military hospital. Fire destroyed the interior of the church in 1794, but it was rebuilt with the original walls. In Zion Church, the official commemorative service following the death of Washington was held under the auspices of Congress on December 26, 1799.

## His Marriage

Peter Muhlenberg had many warm friends among the people of the great Lutheran congregation in Philadelphia. It was thus natural that here he should find the girl of his heart. Early in November 1770, he came down from the Raritan region to Philadelphia, and on the 6th, they were married.

The bride was Anna Barbara Meyer, daughter of Mathias Meyer, a well-to-do potter. She was born in Philadelphia on February 28, 1751, and was baptized on March 10, following by the pastor of Saint Michael's Church.

Though the Reverend Henry Melchior Muhlenberg was still pastor of the Philadelphia congregation, he did not pronounce the words that made his son Peter and Anna Barbara Meyer man and wife. The fact that the record of the marriage is not to be found either in the books of the Philadelphia or the Trappe congregation has hitherto proved somewhat disconcerting to investigators in the minutia of genealogy. But in the books of Saint Michael's Lutheran Church, Germantown, Philadelphia, may be seen the entry of the marriage. It was performed in Philadelphia by the pastor of that church, the Reverend John Frederick Schmidt.

Pastor Schmidt had been educated at the Halle Institutions and had made the acquaintance of the Muhlenberg boys there. It may be that they interested him in America. He arrived in Pennsylvania in 1769, and, after assisting the elder Muhlenberg for some months, he became pastor of the congregation in Germantown, then a village six miles north of the city of Philadelphia and now part of the city. No doubt, Pastor Schmidt was a man after Peter Muhlenberg's own heart. He, too, preached patriotism in the days of the American Revolution, with the result that when the British occupied Germantown and Philadelphia, he had to seek refuge in the interior of Pennsylvania. In 1785, he became one of the pastors of the Philadelphia congregation, and he held that post until his death in 1812.

In the record of her baptism, marriage, and death, the name of Peter Muhlenberg's wife is written "Anna," but usually throughout her life, she was called "Hannah," and she is thus named in the wills of her father and mother. The father, Mathias Meyer, died in the spring of 1775, but the mother, who had been Esther Knoepler, survived until 1801. Besides the daughter Anna, there also was a daughter Mary, who married Andrew Epple. Perhaps Justus Frederick Meyer, who went to England in 1763 on the same ship with Peter Muhlenberg, related to this family.

## A Call from Virginia

A few months after his marriage, Peter Muhlenberg, in May 1771, received a letter from James Wood, justice of the peace in Woodstock, Virginia, which was fraught with grave consequences for the young minister. Squire Wood was in New York when he wrote the letter on May 6. He was looking for a minister to serve in Woodstock; one who could preach both in German and English. In New York, he heard about Peter Muhlenberg's popularity in the Raritan region, where he conducted services at times in the English tongue. The letter of Squire Wood read as follows:

> Reverend Sir: I have been requested by the vestry of a vacant
> charge in Virginia to use my endeavors to find a person of an
> unexceptionable character, either ordained or desirous of obtain-
> ing ordination in the clergy of the Church of England, who
> is capable of preaching both in the English and the German
> languages. The Living, as established by the Laws of the Land,
> with Perquisites is of the value of Two hundred and Fifty pounds
> Pennsylvania currency, with a Parsonage House and a Farm of
> at least Two hundred Acres of Extremely Good Land with every
> other convenient Out House belonging to the same, which will
> render it very convenient for a Gentleman's Seat. And having
> just now received a Character and Information of you from Mr.
> John Vanorden of Brunswick, I am very inclinable to believe
> You would fully answer the expectations of the people of that
> Parish; the Gentleman of whom I have had information does not

know, whether You are ordained by the Bishop of London or not. However, be that as it will, if You can come well recommended to the Vestry, they will recommend You in such a manner as to make Your ordination certain. If You should think those Proposals worth Your acceptance, I shall be glad You would write me an Answer, to be left in Philadelphia at the Sign of the Cross Keys, where I shall stay a few days on my return home, when, if I find You inclined to accept of this Living, You may expect to hear from me, directed to the care of the Gentleman, of whom I have been favored with the information, which I have received.

I am, tho' unacquainted, Reverend Sir, Y. Ob. Serv.,

JAMES WOOD

New York, 4th May, 1771

P. S. If You should determine to go to London, I make no Doubt of the Vestry advancing sufficient Sum to defray the expenses.

For some time, the Lutheran Ministerium of Pennsylvania had been receiving inquiries for ministers to serve the German Lutherans in western Virginia. In search of fertile farmland, the German settlers of Pennsylvania overflowed into the Shenandoah Valley of Virginia. Topographically this region, west of the Alleghenies, differs greatly from the plantation lands of the Virginia seaboard. Following its settlement, the character of the population likewise differed radically from that to the east. Here there were no great manor houses with aristocratic families and splendid entertainment. Instead, the people were much like those of Pennsylvania, tilling farms, or living in villages. Besides the Germans, Scotch Irish also came into the Valley in large numbers and brought with them the Presbyterian church. Among the Germans were adherents of the Lutheran, Reformed, and Brethren faiths, with a few Mennonites. In many communities, German was the dominant language, just as in Pennsylvania. German was spoken to some extent up to the middle of the nineteenth century, and today many families in the Shenandoah Valley have German names.

Situated 150 miles northwest of Richmond and thirty miles south of Winchester, which latter town was at the northern or lower end of the Shenandoah Valley, Woodstock was first known as Muellerstadt, named for Jacob Mueller, who owned 2000 acres thereabouts in the middle of the eighteenth century. Unlike other towns that grew sporadically as houses were built, Muellerstadt was deliberately planned by Mueller in 1761 and laid out in streets and building lots. At about the same time, the Virginia Assembly gave the town the name of Woodstock. It was then in Frederick County. In 1772, this part of Frederick County was constituted into Dunmore County, with Woodstock as the county seat. The new county was named for Lord Dunmore, then the royal governor of Virginia.

The German Lutheran settlers of the Shenandoah Valley were nominally affiliated with the parishes of the established Church of England, which was the only religious denomination having full legal recognition in Virginia.

The parish of which Woodstock was the center was named Beckford Parish. Occasionally Lutheran ministers from eastern Virginia or from Pennsylvania visited the Valley and held services.

Elsewhere in Virginia, there had been much controversy over the question of religious tolerance. The great numbers of Scotch-Irish Presbyterians who poured into the colony indignantly resisted attempts to impose the established church upon them. After the middle of the eighteenth century, many Baptists also came to Virginia. Some preachers of this denomination were thrown into prison for conducting services. The British Toleration Act was the guide in Virginia in matters of worship by "dissenters," but it was variously interpreted at different times.

As Squire Wood indicated in his letter, a clergyman was wanted at Woodstock who could minister to the Germans as well as the English settlers and who should have the ordination of the Church of England, thus averting any doubt as to the validity of his pastoral acts, especially marriages. Strictly construed, the law then in force in Virginia sanctioned no marriage by a "dissenting" minister. Furthermore, as a minister of the established church, his salary would be assured through taxation.

While the Lutheran church of Germany never required ordination by a bishop in the line of the apostolic succession, as was the rule in the

Church of England, Lutheran leaders were not disposed to quibble over the matter, even though they considered it unfair that the Anglican church declared Lutheran ordination invalid. The Swedish Lutheran Church still maintained the apostolic succession in the bishopric, and its clergy was recognized by the Church of England. The Lutherans regarded theological differences between them and the Anglicans as of slight significance. The chief distinction between the two faiths, they felt, was that of language, and there were many Lutherans who saw no reason for trying to establish English Lutheran congregations but were satisfied to have their young people who no longer understood German become members of the Anglican church. Thus, Peter Muhlenberg found no obstacle in the requirement that he should be ordained by a bishop of the Church of England. His father, however, is said to have protested such a step.

Soon after receiving Squire Wood's letter, Peter Muhlenberg visited the Shenandoah Valley. He took with him a cordial letter of recommendation from the Reverend Richard Peters, of the Anglican Church in Philadelphia. The letter described Peter Muhlenberg as "a young and promising divine who is of amiable disposition and has great esteem both among the Lutherans and the English."

The outcome of the visit was the decision by Muhlenberg to accept the call and go to England for ordination, that being necessary as there were no Anglican bishops in America.

## Ordained in the Church of England

Muhlenberg sailed from Philadelphia on March 2, 1772. He recorded in his journal the happenings of his brief stay in England.
Arriving in London, he called on the Lord Bishop of London. The latter's chaplain, the Reverend Dr. Hind, examined Muhlenberg. Two other American candidates for ordination were then in London—William Braidfoot, of Virginia, and William White, of Philadelphia. The latter had already received his deacon's orders. The Bishop of Ely conferred deacon's orders upon Muhlenberg and Braidfoot, which was followed by the private ordination of all three to the priesthood on April 23, 1772, by the

Bishop of London in the King's Chapel at Saint James'. In Muhlenberg's words, on this occasion, the bishop "made a very serious and eloquent sermon." A little later, all three of the newly ordained clergymen went to a theater to see a performance by Garrick. And two of them were from Pennsylvania, in whose principal city the theater was then outlawed.

All three of the men who thus received the holy orders of the Anglican church were among the comparatively small number of clergymen so ordained who supported the cause of the colonies in the Revolution. The Reverend William White, the rector of Christ Church, Philadelphia, was chosen chaplain of the Continental Congress, and after the war, he led the efforts to reorganize the Episcopal church in America. He was one of the first three bishops chosen at a convention held in Wilmington, Delaware, in 1786, and, one of those named declining, Dr. White and the Reverend Samuel Provoost, of New York, were consecrated in London in 1787. Bishop White remained the head of the Diocese of Pennsylvania until his death in 1836. The Reverend William Braidfoot, a native of Scotland, was rector of Portsmouth Parish, Norfolk County, Virginia, when the Revolution opened. He joined the American army as a chaplain, remaining on duty throughout the war. Resuming charge of Portsmouth Parish, he lived only a few years longer.

While in London, Muhlenberg made the acquaintance of members of the Penn family, and he also called on Dr. Ziegenhagen, the German court preacher and friend of the elder Muhlenberg. Dr. Ziegenhagen did not at all approve of the English ordination. On May 3, Peter Muhlenberg preached to a large congregation in the German Chapel in the Savoy. Soon afterward, he sailed for home, and the following autumn, he assumed the duties of his charge in Woodstock.

The question naturally arises: Of what religious denomination was Peter Muhlenberg in Virginia—Lutheran or Episcopal? In the conduct of parish affairs, undoubtedly, the method of the established church in Virginia was followed. He was rector of Beckford Parish, and as such, provision was made for his support by tithes, which the people had to pay. When he conducted services in the English language, probably he adhered to the ritual of the English *Book of Common Prayer*.

But when he held German services, he unquestionably followed the Lutheran practice. This is proved by his manuscript "Agenda," or church liturgy, which has been preserved, and which is a copy of the liturgy that his father had prepared for the German Lutheran churches in 1748.

According to this order of service, which Peter Muhlenberg used in his Virginia parish, there was first the confession of sins and the collect, followed by the reading of the epistle for the day. A hymn was sung, and then the gospel for the day was read. The congregation next joined in a repetition of the creed in versified form, after which another hymn was sung, this being succeeded by the sermon. The elder Muhlenberg was not addicted to excessively long sermons, as were many of the Scotch-Irish Presbyterian preachers. He noted in his "Agenda" that "ordinarily the sermon should be limited to three-quarters of an hour." After the sermon came the general prayers or litany with special petitions for the sick, the Lord's Prayer, and the announcements of matters relating to church affairs. The service closed with the Votum: "The peace of God, which passeth all understanding, keep your hearts and minds, through Christ Jesus, unto eternal life. Amen."

It is interesting to note that Peter Muhlenberg's copy of the "Agenda" contains an addition not in other manuscript copies that exist, for there are no contemporary printed copies. The addition, presumably made by Peter Muhlenberg, reads thus:

> After the sermon and the closing hymn, the pastor goes to the
> altar and says: "The Lord be with you."
> Cong. Resp. "And with thy spirit."
> Pastor. "Let us pray."
> Hold us up, O Lord our God, that we may live; and let our hope
> never make us ashamed. Help us by Thy might, that we may
> wax strong; and so shall we ever delight ourselves in Thy statutes,
> through Jesus Christ, Thy dear Son, our Lord. Amen.

Peter Muhlenberg's copy of the "Agenda" also made provision for concluding the afternoon service with this benediction: "The Lord bless thee and keep thee; the Lord make His face to shine upon thee, and be gracious unto Thee; the Lord lift up his countenance upon thee, and give thee peace, in the name of the Father, and of the Son, and of the Holy Ghost, Amen."

The Lutheran Ministerium of Pennsylvania evidently did not assume that Muhlenberg had abjured Lutheranism by accepting Episcopal ordination and subscribing to the Thirty-Nine Articles of Religion. While he did not attend Ministerium meetings during the few years he remained in Woodstock, yet the Ministerium looked upon him as a Lutheran pastor in good standing, for when, in 1772, a Lutheran minister in Culpeper, Virginia, complained to the Ministerium that the support from his congregation was inadequate and that he needed an assistant for some distant congregations, the Ministerium resolved that a letter be addressed to Peter Muhlenberg, who lived sixty miles from the scene of the complaint, asking that he investigate the matter.

After the Revolution, Peter Muhlenberg was identified with Lutheran congregations in Pennsylvania. In 1787, when the Ministerium decided to apply for a charter, "Peter Muhlenberg, Esq.," was named as one of a committee of seven to procure the charter.

About the time Peter Muhlenberg assumed the Virginia pastorate, a new church was built in Woodstock, replacing a log structure previously used. That preparation for this improvement was begun soon after assurances had been received of his acceptance of the call, is indicated by an advertisement appearing in the *Philadelphia Staatsbote*, a German newspaper, in January 1772, bearing the signatures of Abraham Keller and Lorenz Schnell, vestrymen. The advertisement invited proposals for building two churches in Frederick County, Virginia, in the parish of Beckford, fourteen miles from Winchester, one building to measure thirty-two by thirty-four feet, and the other thirty-four by thirty-six feet.

Abraham Brubacher gave the site for the Woodstock church, bordering on the public square in the center of the town and situated opposite the courthouse.

While at Woodstock, Muhlenberg also held occasional services in Winchester, Strasburg, and Rude's Hill.

Gloria Dei Church in Philadelphia, Pennsylvania

Saint Michael's German Lutheran Church, in Philadelphia, Pennsylvania

Zion Lutheran Church in Philadelphia, Pennsylvania

Bishop William White

King's Chapel at Saint James' Cathedral, London, England

# III

## SERVICE IN THE REVOLUTION

### A Leader in the Patriot Cause

In 1772, the year when Muhlenberg began his Woodstock pastorate, John Murray, Earl of Dunmore, became royal governor of Virginia, and his name was given to the new county created that year with Woodstock as the county seat. Opposition toward Great Britain had gradually been gaining strength in Virginia, since the time of the Stamp Act of 1765, when Patrick Henry had vehemently denounced that law in the House of Burgesses. Henry's eloquence served to keep alive the antagonism toward Great Britain, for, though the Stamp Act was repealed after a year, Parliament insisted upon its right to tax the American colonists by imposing new duties on glass, paper, and tea. Previous royal governors had sought to be conciliatory and were not personally distasteful to the Virginians. But Dunmore's policy was to rule by authority and force.

Following the destruction of the tea in Boston Harbor, in December 1773, to protest the tea tax, Parliament ordered the port of Boston closed on and after June 4, 1774. When this news reached Virginia, the Assembly, in session in Williamsburg, the capital, designated June 1 as a day of fasting, humiliation, and prayer for divine interposition to avert "the heavy calamity which threatens the civil rights of America." Thereupon, on May 28, Lord Dunmore dissolved the Assembly because its action in designating the day of prayer reflected upon the King and Parliament.

Just about that time, the governor's wife and children arrived in Williamsburg from New York, and prior to dissolution, the Assembly arranged to welcome them at a ball in the capitol on the night of May 26. The ball took place, notwithstanding cordial relations between Dunmore and the Assembly were at a breaking point.

The following day the members of the Assembly, termed burgesses, met in the Raleigh Tavern, Williamsburg, adopted a resolution against the use of tea, directed a Committee of Correspondence to propose that a general congress of the American colonies be held and recommended the elected of delegates in the counties of Virginia to a convention on August 1 to determine upon the future course of the colony.

The Committee of Correspondence had already been functioning for almost a year, maintaining contact with the other colonies. Massachusetts had spoken in favor of a congress of the colonies even before Virginia, though that action was not known in Virginia when the burgesses met on May 27. The outcome of the suggestions was the assembling of the Continental Congress in Philadelphia.

The day of fasting, humiliation, and prayer was generally observed in Virginia on June 1, and the people went to church attired in mourning. No doubt that day, Peter Muhlenberg conducted the service in the Woodstock church.

What occurred on June 1 in Woodstock may be a matter of conjecture. But not what occurred on June 16. On that day, in accordance with the recommendation of the members of the Assembly in session in the Raleigh Tavern, the people of Dunmore County met in Woodstock to define their attitude as to the great issues raised between the American colonies and the mother country. By this time, Peter Muhlenberg was recognized not only as the spiritual but also as the civic leader of the people of the Woodstock region. He held the office of magistrate. At the meeting on June 16, he was chosen moderator—that is, presiding officer—and was made the chairman of the Committee on Resolutions.

The committee quickly submitted resolutions, modeled after those adopted at a similar meeting in Frederick County. In part, they set forth:

■ That we will pay due submission to such acts of government as his Majesty has a right by law to exercise over his subjects, and to such only.

■ That it is in the inherent right of British subjects to be governed and taxed by representatives chosen by themselves only, and that every act of the British Parliament respecting the internal policy of America is a dangerous and unconstitutional invasion of our rights and privileges.

■ That the enforcing the execution of the said act of Parliament by a military power will have a necessary tendency to cause a civil war, thereby dissolving that union which has so long happily subsisted between the mother country and her colonies; and that we will most heartily and unanimously concur with our suffering and brethren of Boston and every other part of North America that may be the immediate victim of tyranny, in promoting all proper measures to avert such dreadful calamities, to procure a redress of our grievances and to secure our common liberties.

The resolutions further contained promises not to import goods from England nor to export goods to that country, pledging support "to each other and to our country" and authorizing the appointment of a Committee of Safety and Correspondence, as was being done generally in other counties. The members of this committee for Dunmore County were the Reverend Peter Muhlenberg, chairman; Francis Slaughter; Abraham Bird; Taverner Beale; John Tipton; and Abraham Bowman.

Some time afterward, in accordance with the action of the Virginia burgesses, in their Raleigh Tavern meeting, two delegates were elected to represent Dunmore County in the convention called to meet in Williamsburg on August 1. The delegates chosen, as their names stand on the role of the convention, were "Jonathan Clarke, Esq., and Peter

Muhlenberg, Clerk." The term "clerk" here was used in the old sense, meaning a cleric or priest.

The convention was duly opened in Williamsburg on Monday, August 1, 1774, and remained in session throughout the week until Saturday, the 6th. Muhlenberg and Clarke were present, and they supported Patrick Henry in his demands for vigorous action, which demands were not always approved by the convention. Colonel George Washington also was a member of this convention, representing Fairfax County, and he made a speech offering to raise and subsist 1000 men and march with them to the aid of Boston.

A declaration which the convention adopted opened with the words, "We his Majesty's dutiful and loyal subjects, the delegates of the freeholders of Virginia." It was agreed not to import goods from Great Britain after November 1, nor to import slaves from any place. Exports to Great Britain were to cease, and no tea was to be used so long as it was taxed. The members obligated themselves to take measures to improve the breed of sheep in Virginia to increase the production of wool. Merchants were warned not to take advantage of commercial conditions to increase prices of commodities. Instructions for the delegates to the Continental Congress in Philadelphia were also adopted.

From Williamsburg, Peter Muhlenberg probably went to Philadelphia. The diary of his father records that the son was in Philadelphia toward the end of August, when his parents left on a voyage to South Carolina and Georgia, and that Peter Muhlenberg reported to his father relative to conditions among the Lutherans of Culpeper County, Virginia, in accordance with a request of the Ministerium two years before. It may be that Peter Muhlenberg remained in Philadelphia long enough to witness the opening of the Continental Congress on September 5, in Carpenters' Hall, Philadelphia, when Peyton Randolph, of Virginia, was chosen the first President of Congress.

Muhlenberg was subjected to criticism, especially from the clergy of the established church, because of his political activity. Toward the end of the year 1774, he seemed to have felt it advisable to withdraw from civic responsibilities, for on January 17, 1775, he wrote to one of his brothers:

The times are getting troublesome with us, and begin to wear a
hostile appearance. Independent companies are forming in every
county, and politics engross all conversation. I had thrown up my
commission as chairman of the Committee of Correspondence,
and of magistrate likewise; but last week we had a general election
in the county for a great committee, according to the resolves of
Congress, and I am again chosen chairman, so that, whether I
choose or not, I am to be a politician.

The convention, now virtually the governing body of Virginia, met
again on March 20, 1775, in Richmond, Peyton Randolph presiding,
and again the delegates from Dunmore County were Jonathan Clarke
and Peter Muhlenberg. The sessions were held in Saint John's Church.
It was at these meetings that Patrick Henry delivered his impassioned
appeal, closing with the memorable words, "As for me, give me liberty or
give me death."

The resolutions adopted in response to Henry's oratory set forth the
desires of the convention for peace, but agreed nevertheless "that the
colony immediately be put into a position of defense," that the militia
should be organized and drilled in every county and that steps be taken
to encourage the manufacture of salt, gunpowder, iron, and steel, all of
which had hitherto been imported.

The following month, Lord Dunmore had the powder removed from
the public magazine in Williamsburg, and immediately there was alarm
and denunciation among the patriots. Patrick Henry mustered a force of
volunteers who were marching upon the capital when Dunmore agreed
to pay a sum of money in compensation for the powder.

Meanwhile, a series of troubles due to Indian hostilities on the Virginia frontier had further incensed the people about Dunmore, for there
were grave suspicions that he had fomented the attacks by the Indians
on the settlers for diverting the attention of the populace from their
grievances against Great Britain and uniting them against the natives.
Convincing evidence soon appeared that the policy of Great Britain in

dealing with her troublesome colonies included the use of the Indians in warfare upon the frontiers.

Early in 1775, the British Parliament took some steps toward conciliation, and following instructions along this line, Lord Dunmore summoned the Virginia Assembly to convene in Williamsburg on June 1, 1775. To a large extent, the membership of the Assembly was the same as that of the preceding conventions. The minutes of the session beginning June 1, however, contain no mention of Muhlenberg's name. Peyton Randolph was the speaker. The proceedings of the Continental Congress and the Virginia convention were reported to the Assembly, and in response to the conciliatory offers of Parliament, a statement prepared by Thomas Jefferson was adopted rejecting these offers because they did not go far enough.

Sensing the attitude of the Assembly, Dunmore and his family left Williamsburg and took refuge on a British ship at Yorktown. Then the final session of the Virginia Assembly under royal rule was terminated with a call for a meeting of the convention in July.

Muhlenberg and Clarke continued to represent their county in the convention. There was a further session in Richmond on December 1, 1775, which adjourned to meet in Williamsburg on the 4th. On December 8, the convention took under consideration a proclamation by Lord Dunmore declaring martial law in Virginia, calling upon all men capable of bearing arms to resort to his Majesty's standard in Norfolk or be considered traitors and declaring free all negro slaves and indentured servants of rebels. The proclamation was referred to a committee of ten members, of whom Peter Muhlenberg was one, the committee being instructed to prepare a reply and to select for publication certain letters before the convention pertaining to the crisis now at hand.

## The Pastor Becomes a Colonel

Altogether the matters referred to this committee were the most important questions before the convention. The committee presented its report on December 13, and it was unanimously adopted. The reply which the committee had prepared declared Dunmore's proclamation violated the constitution and laws, assuming powers which even the King could not exercise. Therefore, the reply continued, the people were "compelled by a disagreeable but absolute necessity of repelling force to maintain our just rights and privileges, and we appeal to God, who is the sovereign disposer of all events, for the justice of our cause, trusting to his unerring wisdom and direct our councils and give success to our arms."

Two battalions of troops had already been organized. The convention now decided to enlist six more battalions, and it was specified that one was to be composed of Germans and German officers. Peter Muhlenberg also served on several other committees of the convention dealing with problems arising out of the Indian incursions.

The sessions of the convention continued into January 1776. On January 12, the appointment of officers for the new battalions was announced. The word "battalion" as then used signified a regiment in command of a colonel, not a unit in a regiment, as it meant later. The Eighth Battalion was the German command for which provision had been made. The colonel chosen for it was the Woodstock parson, Peter Muhlenberg.

All the other colonels, except Patrick Henry, commander of the First Battalion, had been engaged in military service in the British army or with colonial commands in the French and Indian War. They were also older than Muhlenberg, who was then 29. No doubt, it was known that in his youthful days, he also had been for a short time in the British army, though his experience as a secretary at that time hardly counted for much in fitting him to command a battalion. It was rather his inherent capacity for leadership, especially among the Germans, that entitled him to the place.

General George Washington and Patrick Henry, it has been said, both urged Muhlenberg's appointment. There are traditions that Washington had made the acquaintance of Muhlenberg while visiting the Shenandoah Valley and that they had hunted deer together. However, Washington was not in Virginia then, being then occupied with his duties as commander of the American army near Boston.

Besides Muhlenberg, the officers of the Eighth Battalion were Abraham Bowman, lieutenant colonel, and Peter Helfenstein, major. As the names indicate, both were from German families. Abraham Bowman had served with Muhlenberg on the Committee of Safety and Correspondence for Dunmore County.

Peter Muhlenberg had now decided that there was a greater need for his service in the American army than in the pulpit. He went home to Woodstock, and soon the news spread that the parson would preach his farewell sermon. Though the tradition of that sermon is definite and unquestioned, yet there is no record of the date when it was preached. Likely, it was in January 1776.

Not only did the assembled throng fill every bit of space in the church on this momentous Sunday, but it overflowed upon the surrounding burial ground. Clad as usual in the black ministerial robe of his church, Muhlenberg once more—and for the last time—repeated the liturgy which his father had prepared and which the son had copied with his own hand. The substance of the sermon is preserved only through tradition. Though its text and exact language are now lost, with such a speaker and such an environment, it surely was a stirring discourse.

A narrative of the occasion written by Henry A. Muhlenberg seventy years later quoted Pastor Muhlenberg as saying that "in the language of the Holy Writ there is a time for all things, a time to preach and a time to pray, but those times have passed away. There is a time to fight, and that time has now come." Then, after pronouncing the benediction, he removed his clerical robe and stood before his congregation in the uniform of a Virginia colonel. One account says the assemblage arose and sang Luther's hymn, "*Ein Feste Burg* [A Mighty Fortress Is Our God]." The author who tells this, Herrmann Schuricht, also asserts that though Muhlenberg wore his military uniform under his ministerial garb while conducting service, he did not buckle on his sword until after he had removed his robe. Recruiting for the German battalion was begun at once, and the names of several hundred men of the parish were enrolled.

Whether or not Peter Muhlenberg went to the pulpit that day with his military uniform concealed under his pastoral robes is lost to history, but there are no contemporary accounts of this dramatic event. Historians since have labeled this the "Muhlenberg Myth" and cite the lack of sources besides the potentially embellished version from a descendent. Additionally, it would be highly improper for a clergyman to do so within the confines of the church. It is more likely he gave a stirring sermon and then left his post as pastor to take charge of his unit later.

The assumption usually is that Muhlenberg's allusion to "a time for all things" was a quotation from the Scriptures. The words as given do not appear in the Bible, though the thought is found in the third chapter of Ecclesiastes:

> To every thing there is a season,
> and a time to every purpose under heaven:
>
> . . . . . . . . . . . . . . . . . .
>
> A time to kill, and a time to heal;
> A time to break down, and a time to build up;
> A time to weep, and a time to laugh;
> A time to mourn, and a time to dance;
> A time to cast away stones, and a time to gather stones together;
> A time to embrace, and a time to refrain from embracing;
> A time to get, and a time to lose;
> A time to keep and a time to cast away;
> A time to rend, and a time to sew;
> A time to keep silence, and a time to speak;
> A time to love, and a time to hate;
> A time of war, and a time of peace.

There is a reason to believe that Peter Muhlenberg realized what today would be termed the publicity value of his sermon in stimulating recruiting and that he repeated the sermon with its dramatic finale at Rude's Hill, near New Market.

A black silk robe, much frayed, in the Krauth Memorial Library of the Philadelphia Lutheran Theological Seminary, Mount Airy, is said to be the identical robe which Peter Muhlenberg discarded. It has been loaned to the library by Elon O. Henkel of New Market, Virginia. The robe had been in the Henkel family for many years, having come down from the Reverend Paul Henkel, an early Lutheran minister in the Shenandoah Valley.

## A Theme for Poets

The incident in the church in Woodstock was a favorite theme for poets and story writers for many years. In most of these patriotic productions, whether prose or verse, poetic license has been exercised to the utmost. Sometimes muddled writers have portrayed the scene as taking place in old Augustus Church, Trappe, where Peter Muhlenberg's father was the pastor since that church is so conspicuously connected with the name of Muhlenberg. At least two drams have dealt with the subject: Dr. Victor Precht's "*Keurass and Kutte* [Cuirass and Cowl"—and Dr. Karl Dilthey's "Robe and Armor." The latter was presented in 1877 in the Germania Theater, New York City.

Of the poems based on the episode, the best known is Thomas Buchanan Read's, which was a long favorite among elocutionists and appeared in most school "readers."

Read, who was born in Chester County, Pennsylvania, not more than twenty-five miles south of Peter Muhlenberg's birthplace, was at the height of his fame as a poet about the time of the Civil War, and he rendered valuable service to the cause of the Union by stimulating patriotic ardor through the medium of his writings. Often, he visited army camps and recited his poems to the soldiers, and all through the North, his verse was reprinted in newspapers and presented at patriotic assemblages. Read's two most famous poems, "The Revolutionary Rising" and "Sheridan's Ride," were products of that period. The scenes of both were in Shenandoah Valley.

Of "Sheridan's Ride," it has been said that it made Sheridan's reputation, though calm investigation, indicates that his ability was much overrated.

But when Read drew the picture of Muhlenberg enrolling his Virginia parishioners for service in the war for independence, he did no violence to the facts. It is true there is mention of the pastor's "snowy locks," though Muhlenberg was not yet thirty years old. But that can be forgiven because of the necessity of finding a rhyme for "flocks."

There is ample verification that Read's poem justly represents the scene when it runs thus:

> The pastor rose; the prayer was strong;
> The psalm was warrior David's song;
> The text, a few short words of might –
> 'The Lord of hosts shall arm the right!'
> He spoke of wrongs too long endured,
> Of sacred rights to be secured,
> Then from the patriot tongue of flame
> The startling words for Freedom came.
> The stirring sentences he spake
> Compelled the heart to glow or quake,
> And, rising on his theme's broad wing,
> And grasping in his nervous hand
> The imaginary battle brand,
> In face of death, he dared to fling
> Defiance to a tyrant king.
>
> Even as he spoke, his frame, renewed,
> In eloquence of attitude,
> Rose, as it seemed, a shoulder higher;
> Then swept his kindling glance of fire
> From startled pew to breathless choir;
> When suddenly his mantle wide
> His hands impatient flung aside,
> And, lo! he met their wondering eyes
> Complete in all a warrior's guise.
>
> 'Who dares' – this was the patriot's cry,
> As striding from the desk, he came –
> 'Come out with me in Freedom's name,
> For her to live, for her to die?'
> A hundred voices answered, 'I!'

## The German Regiment in Service

The recruiting of the German regiment was completed in March 1776. Its officers and men were almost without exception from German families of the Shenandoah Valley. On March 21, the regiment marched for Suffolk in southeastern Virginia. Lord Dunmore, on a warship in the Chesapeake Bay near Norfolk, had collected a force of Tories, who, together with the men from the ships, raided the coast towns from time to time, burned Norfolk and captured Portsmouth. The newly recruited troops of Virginia were assembled about Norfolk and Portsmouth, with the purpose of driving Dunmore and his force out of the country.

On April 3, 1776, Colonel Muhlenberg, Lieutenant Colonel Bowman, and Major Helfenstein, of the Eighth, or German, Regiment, appeared before the Virginia Committee of Safety, in Williamsburg, and subscribed to the articles of war and their oath of office, after which they received their commissions as officers, dated March 1.

The adjutant of the regiment was Francis Swaine, whose wife was Mary Catherine, a sister of Peter Muhlenberg. The Swaines were living in Woodstock when the war began, and Swaine joined the regiment. When Muhlenberg was promoted to brigadier general, Swaine became brigade major. After the war, he held numerous civic offices in Montgomery County and elsewhere in Pennsylvania.

The Reverend Christian Streit, a Lutheran minister and a friend of the Muhlenbergs, became chaplain of the regiment. Streit was a native of the Raritan region, in northern New Jersey, where Peter Muhlenberg had his first pastorate, and after being licensed to preach, in 1769, he served the Lutheran congregation in Easton, Pennsylvania.

The colors of the regiment consisted of a salmon-colored silk banner and a broad fringe of the same hue. In the center was a scroll inscribed, "VIII Virga Regt."

In formulating its plan of campaign against the "rebels" in America, the British ministry contemplated a strong movement for the subjugation of the southern colonies in 1776. In January, General Henry Clinton and some troops set sail from Boston. Off the coast of North Carolina, near the Cape Fear River, the squadron waited for the arrival of more troops from England.

The command of the American forces in the South was given to General Charles Lee. Lee had been an officer in the British army in the French and Indian War and in European campaigns. He was able, brilliant, and erratic. Becoming dissatisfied with the British service, he came to America to join the army opposed to Great Britain. Experienced soldiers such as he were few among the Americans, and consequently, he at once gained a high command.

Clinton received a reinforcement of 3000 troops in April. He had several warships, in addition to thirty vessels carrying troops. Nevertheless, the month of May passed without action on his part.

Lord Dunmore continued his desultory warfare along the Virginia coast until July 1776, when he left for New York and went thence to England. Before his departure, in May 1776, the Virginia Convention had directed its delegates to the Continental Congress to propose that that body "declare the United Colonies free and independent states," had also adopted a Declaration of Rights and a state constitution and elected Patrick Henry governor.

General Lee assembled Virginia and North Carolina troops at Wilmington, North Carolina, in the spring of 1776. Muhlenberg's regiment constituted part of this army. Nothing noteworthy occurred, and toward the end of May, the British fleet sailed away.

## In South Carolina and Georgia

The people of Charleston, South Carolina, feared the purpose of the British was to try to capture the city, and Lee was urged to send aid. He doubted that Clinton was going farther south, suspecting the departure from North Carolina might be only a ruse to induce the American army to forsake that locality. However, he sent Muhlenberg's regiment and 700 additional men to Charleston. He himself accompanied the detachment.

Soon it transpired that Charleston was indeed to receive Clinton's attention, for his fleet arrived before the city on June 4.

Again, Clinton's dilatory tactics proved advantageous to the Americans. Militia assembled, and by the end of June, Lee had 5000 men. Sullivan's Island, in the harbor, was fortified, ramparts being built of spongy palmetto logs that resisted bullets and even cannonballs.

After marching for a month, Muhlenberg and his command arrived at Charleston on June 23, 1776. On the 28th, the British warships began a bombardment of Sullivan's Island. Though the fort had only 300 men and twelve cannons, the defenders suffered little, thanks to the protection of the palmetto logs  At this time, occurred one of the heroic incidents of the Revolution. The flagstaff of the fort was shot away when Sergeant Jasper leaped over the ramparts, seized the flag, and fastened it to a sponge staff, which he planted upon the fortifications.

Under cover of the bombardment, the British endeavored to land troops. This brought Muhlenberg's men and several other regiments into action, and the British were driven back to their ships.

General Lee was astonished by the bravery of the untrained American soldiers, about whose valor he had hitherto held no high opinion. His reports on the engagement were full of praise for the men. The bombardment of the fort continued until 11 o'clock at night, but the garrison, under Colonel William Moultrie, Lee informed the president of the Virginia Convention, were "brave to the last degree." As to the repulse of the two attempts of the British to land troops, Lee wrote thus of the Virginia and North Carolina command that achieved this result: "I know not which corps I have the greatest reason to be pleased with, Muhlenberg's Virginians or the North Carolina troops; they were both equally alert, zealous, and spirited."

Thus far, Muhlenberg's regiment was nothing more than a detachment of Virginia militia. Having demonstrated its military capacity, it was now proposed to take the regiment into the Continental Army, but objections were offered that it was not yet at full strength required by the regulations. Discussing this question, General Lee wrote on August 2 that the regiment lacked only forty men of the maximum number, and he continued: "Muhlenberg's regiment was not only the most complete of the province, but I believe of the whole continent. It was not only the most complete in numbers but the best armed, clothed, and equipped for immediate service."

The outcome was that on August 12, Congress passed a resolution taking the Eighth Virginia Regiment into the Continental service, with pay from May 27, when it marched out of Virginia.

Effectively repulsed at Charleston, the British fleet returned to New York.

General Lee now turned his attention to a vexatious problem arising from the presence of British forces in East Florida, which made raids into Georgia. The people of Savannah especially were fearful of a descent upon their city from this quarter, and a delegation of citizens of that place came to Charleston and conferred with Lee. The feasibility of a military movement against the British in Saint Augustine was discussed, and the plan received Lee's approval.

Lee assembled the North Carolina and Virginia troops of his command and told them a secret expedition was being planned in which there would be little danger while the prospects of booty were large. Troops volunteering for this service would be entitled to the booty, and he would give his own share of the plunder for distribution among the soldiers. All the Virginia and South Carolina men at Charleston agreed to accompany Lee in the contemplated campaign. South Carolina troops also joined.

The march to Georgia was made in August at a time when health conditions were at their worst. The army arrived at Savannah on August 17, and on the 22nd, Muhlenberg's regiment and some of the South Carolina troops moved on to Sunbury, on the Newport River, forty-five miles southeast of Savannah, while the remainder were strung out between Savannah and Sunbury. Boats, stores, and provisions were lacking. The sickness became alarming. Nearly every officer was incapacitated. At Sunbury, twelve to fifteen men died daily.

Lee was recalled to the North because of the operations near New York. The Florida expedition was abandoned, and Lee left Savannah early September, directing the North Carolina and Virginia commands to follow.

The northward march of the Virginians was slow. Because so many were sick, the battalions could not proceed in one detachment, but some had to delay along the route to try to regain their strength. Muhlenberg, with the first details, was back in Virginia on December 20. That day he wrote his father in Trappe describing the devastation in his command due to sickness and death. The regiment, he said, had orders to proceed to New York to join Washington's army.

Muhlenberg himself suffered all his life from the consequences of the disease contracted on the futile Georgia campaign. Major Helfenstein, of his regiment, died after returning to Virginia.

Before joining the Continental Army, it was necessary to recruit the regiment. On January 21, 1777, Congress instructed Muhlenberg to send each company on to the army as soon as its ranks were full. The last detachment of the regiment was detained farther south until February.

Up to February 1777, Colonel Muhlenberg was stationed in Fredericksburg, Virginia, pursuing his recruiting duties. Since his was a German regiment, he wrote to the Council of the state that he believed he could gain more men if his headquarters were in Winchester, in the Shenandoah Valley, where the men already in the regiment could not only see friends and relatives before leaving for the North but could also stimulate enlistment. Permission to make the change was granted.

## Promotion to Brigadier General

Recognizing Muhlenberg's capable service in the southern campaign, Congress, on February 1, 1777, promoted him to brigadier general. His last official act as colonel of the German Regiment was to suggest to General Washington that the men were equipped with muskets instead of the rifles they then had, saying that because they were so continually exposed to the weather the rifles often were unserviceable, whereas muskets were not subject to that disadvantage. The parson had now become an expert in armament.

As brigadier general, Muhlenberg was assigned to the command of all Continental forces in Virginia, with instructions to complete the recruiting of the different regiments as quickly as possible and send them to Washington's army, in northern New Jersey. In April 1777, the First, Fifth, Ninth, and Thirteenth Virginia Regiments were designated as the units of Muhlenberg's Brigade.

Early in May, General Muhlenberg reported to Washington, commander-in-chief of the American army, in his headquarters in Morristown, New Jersey. The army then occupied its fortified winter camp on the heights of Middlebrook. He formally took command of his brigade on May 26. His brigade and that of General George Weedon, also consisting of Virginia regiments, composed the division under Major General Nathanael Greene.

The old German Regiment of Virginia did not arrive in camp until June. The colonel of that regiment now was Baron Henry Leonard Philip de Arendt.

Following the disastrous campaign of 1776 near New York, the American army had been forced to retreat southward through New Jersey and then into Pennsylvania. The victorious British, with their German auxiliary troops, held possession of New York and looked forward to the early capture of the rebel capital, Philadelphia. By his Christmas raid upon the German troops in Trenton and the ensuing American triumph at Princeton, Washington rescued the American cause from despair. In the winter and spring of 1777, the army spent about Morristown in northern New Jersey.

Now summer was at hand. Minor skirmishes with the British followed. Then on July 23, British General Howe with his army, sailed out of New York harbor in the ships of his brother, Admiral Richard Howe, which maneuver was destined to puzzle Washington for some weeks and result in the Pennsylvania campaign of 1777.

After waiting nearly a week without hearing anything as to the destination of the British, Washington, fearing Philadelphia, capital of the new nation, was threatened, slowly advanced his army across New Jersey toward the Delaware River. Yet all the time, the American commander wondered whether Howe was not executing a feint to draw the Americans away from New York. General John Burgoyne, with an army of British and Germans, was moving south from Canada into New York, and the reasonable course seemed to be for Howe to co-operate with Burgoyne.

Greene's division, which Muhlenberg's brigade was a part, arrived at Coryell's Ferry, on the Delaware River, now New Hope, Bucks County, Pennsylvania, on the night of July 29. The troops at once began crossing the river, and on the 31st, they marched down York Road in the direction of Philadelphia. That day Washington was informed the British fleet, to the number of two hundred and twenty-eight sail, had been seen at the Delaware Capes. Washington and his staff pressed on to Philadelphia, arriving there that night. But the army went into camp near Little Neshaminy Creek, near Hartsville, Bucks County.

At Philadelphia, Washington learned to his astonishment that after hovering about the Delaware Capes for several days, the British fleet had sailed out to sea. Once more, he was beset by uncertainty, suspecting his first thought of a strategy to draw him away from New York might have been the truth.

However, on August 1, the American army resumed its march down York Road, crossed westward through Germantown, and went into camp between Germantown and Falls of Schuylkill, upon an elevated site overlooking Philadelphia. Here the army remained until August 8.

On the first Sunday in the camp, General Muhlenberg issued this order: "The Rev'd Mr. Tate will perform divine service this afternoon at 5 o'clock; the captains will see that all men not on duty to attend and behave properly."

As information about the enemy was still lacking, the army on the 8th returned to its old campground on the Little Neshaminy in Bucks County to be prepared to proceed toward New York should it transpire that Howe really intended to help Burgoyne.

It was a period of intense heat. Upon arriving at camp, General Muhlenberg directed the men of his brigade "to fix booths before their tents to shelter them from the heat."

Sutlers selling liquor caused trouble here and at other camps. The officers of General Muhlenberg's brigade were summoned to meet on August 22 "at the tavern at the Cross Roads" to consider the sutlers' prices for liquor.

Evidently, a disposition to go foraging developed among the soldiers, for on August 13, General Washington requested General Muhlenberg "to order a guard over Mr. Miller's oats, to consist of a sergeant and ten men."

Lafayette, Pulaski, and other military men who recently arrived from Europe joined the army at the Neshaminy camp. They were a source of embarrassment to Washington, for most of them claimed high posts and good pay. No doubt it was the arrival of these Europeans that caused Washington to incorporate the following in the general orders for August 13: "Two sober, honest lads who are to talk French are to be sent to headquarters this afternoon at 6 o'clock. General Muhlenberg will send one from his brigade, and General Charles Scott another, if to be found in their brigades."

At last, on August 22 came word that the British fleet was in the Chesapeake Bay. Rather than undertake to pass the American fortifications along the Delaware River, Howe had continued his voyage into the Chesapeake Bay, with the intention of approaching Philadelphia from the rear.

Now there could be no further delay. On the 23rd, the American army broke camp and marched down York Road, encamping that night at Nicetown, below Germantown, General Washington making his headquarters in Stenton, the Logan homestead. The name of the estate evidently was not familiar to Muhlenberg. His orderly book record for August 23 is headed "Headquarters, Santown, near Germantown."

To cheer and encourage the alarmed inhabitants of Philadelphia, Washington arranged to parade his army through the city the following day, Sunday. He gave detailed directions for attaining the best effect with the limited number of men and the poor equipment at his command. It was a marked tribute to General Muhlenberg that he and his Virginia brigade were instructed to lead the line, preceded only by a troop of cavalry.

## The Battle of Brandywine

The army, now numbering about 11,000 men, proceeding into Delaware to oppose the British, who were debarking 17,000 men from their ships at Elk River, Delaware.

For two weeks, the opposing armies lay within eight or ten miles of each other, and several skirmishes occurred. Seeing he was not favorably stationed to intercept Howe's progress toward Philadelphia, Washington, on September 9, moved his forces northward, across the Pennsylvania line, taking post south of Brandywine Creek, at Chadds Ford. This ford was on one of the main highways to Philadelphia. Here on the banks of the Brandywine, on September 11, 1777, was fought the battle which decided the fate of Philadelphia. It was the first battle of consequence in which Muhlenberg's Virginia troops had a part.

General Wilhelm von Knyphausen's Hessian troops first attacked the Americans at the ford. As Washington massed his regiments here to protect the ford, Lord Charles Cornwallis, with a large part of the British army, made a wide detour westward and northward, crossed the Brandywine at fords far up the stream and thus could menace the American rear. Washington hastily reformed his lines to face Cornwallis, and this part of the battle was fought about old Birmingham Friends' Meeting House. The Americans were forced to fall back.

At this juncture, Muhlenberg's brigade, together with the other Virginia brigade of Weedon, rendered service of incalculable value by holding back the British advance long enough to permit the badly battered American regiments to retire from the meeting house toward Dilworthtown. At one time, Muhlenberg's men alone, after having marched four miles in forty minutes, faced all of Cornwallis' army, and their commander led them in desperate hand-to-hand bayonet fighting. This fortitude of the Virginians prevented the defeat from becoming a rout, for by stemming the onrush of the British, it became possible for the American commanders to check their men and bring about an orderly retreat to the neighborhood of Chester. Muhlenberg's brigade was the last to leave the field of battle.

One of the traditions of the Battle of Brandywine relates that certain Hessian soldiers with the British army recognized Muhlenberg when he charged at the head of his brigade, remembering him from the time they were associated with him in the German army. Whereupon, they shouted: "*Hier kommt Teufel Pete* [Here comes Devil Pete]." This is probably one of the various apocryphal tales which gained popular circulation because it tended to picture Peter Muhlenberg as an audacious and reckless fighter, the peer of that other favorite Pennsylvania warrior who was dubbed "Mad Anthony" Wayne. The Muhlenberg take hardly bears analysis. For one thing, the Hessians were fighting at Chadds Ford and did not accompany Cornwallis. Muhlenberg charged against Cornwallis' troops, not against the Hessians. Furthermore, Muhlenberg never served in the German army. When he ran away from an unhappy apprenticeship in Lubeck, he joined a British regiment that was being recruited in that free city. In this regiment, for the short time he was with it, his duties were those of a secretary, and secretaries are usually not of the swashbuckler type. Of course, there might have been some Hessians in that regiment, and that regiment might have been in Cornwallis' detachment. But the whole story seems improbable.

While it was generally recognized that the service of Muhlenberg's brigade at Brandywine was of the highest importance, yet no special mention thereof appeared in Washington's official report on the battle. It is said some officers complained to General Greene, Muhlenberg's immediate superior, about this omission and that Greene expostulated with Washington, whereupon Washington explained that it was known that Greene was a favorite of Washington, and moreover Muhlenberg's men came from Washington's own state; hence he hesitated about according either the general or the Virginia troops special mention in his reports lest he might be charged with partiality. Washington seems to have adopted a similar course regarding other engagements in which Virginia commands had a prominent part.

## Wartime Experiences at Trappe

At his home in Trappe, twenty-five miles from the Brandywine battlefield, Peter Muhlenberg's father, the Reverend Henry Melchior Muhlenberg, wrote in his journal on the day of the battle that he "heard hard and long-continued cannonading." The following day, learning of the defeat of the Americans and the impending British invasion, he closed his record thus: "Now, Pennsylvania, bend the neck and supplicate the Lord thy God."

The American army fell back to its former campground north of Schuylkill, between Falls of Schuylkill and Germantown, and the authorities of Pennsylvania made desperate efforts to bring more militia into the field.

Purposing to give battle once more before permitting Philadelphia to fall into the hands of the foe, Washington advanced into Chester County. Rain, which dampened the powder, prevented collision with the British. The two armies maneuvered throughout northern Chester County until September 19, when the Americans crossed to the north side of the Schuylkill, camping for a short time near the home of the Muhlenbergs, at Trappe. On the 21st, the British also crossed the Schuylkill. Washington retired westward to the vicinity of Pottstown, and the way was open to the British to take possession of Philadelphia, which they did on September 26.

There was great distress and alarm all through southwestern Pennsylvania. Congress, government officials, and many families fled from Philadelphia. Throngs of fugitives passed up the Reading Road past the Muhlenberg home at Trappe. The wife and child of Peter Muhlenberg were then living in the Trappe parsonage, having arrived in a wagon on September 10. Three days later, Peter's brother Henry, also a Lutheran minister, arrived from Philadelphia with his wife. Another brother, Frederick, had been at Trappe for some time and was assisting his father in his pastoral work, usually preaching in the New Hanover church. On September 15, the Muhlenberg house had eighteen occupants. The daughter,

Margaret Henrietta, who had married the Reverend John C. Kunze, remained in Philadelphia with her husband during the British occupation, the husband being the pastor of the Lutheran congregation in that city.

Sometime before this, the unpleasant news arrived that Francis Swaine, son-in-law of Pastor Muhlenberg, who was brigade major in Peter Muhlenberg's brigade, had been convicted by court-martial of charges of neglect of duty, particularly in leaving sick soldiers exposed at the time the army was in Delaware. He was sentenced to be reprimanded in general orders. After the sentence was executed, Swaine resigned from the army. Later he was state clothier of Pennsylvania, in charge of contracts for supplying the Pennsylvania militia with uniforms, and after the war, he was a brigadier general of the Philadelphia militia.

Respecting the movements of the American army at and near Trappe, the Reverend Henry Melchior Muhlenberg wrote in his journal on September 19:

> We had news that the British troops on the other side of the
> Schuylkill had marched down toward Providence, and with a
> telescope, we could see their camp. In consequence of this Ameri-
> can army, four miles from us forded the Schuylkill breast-high
> and came upon the Philadelphia Road at Augustus Church.
> His Excellency, General Washington, was with the troops in
> person, who marched past here to the Perkiomen.
>
> The procession lasted the whole night, and we had numerous
> visits from officers, wet breast-high, who had to march in this
> condition the whole night, cold and damp as it was, and to bear
> hunger and thirst at the same time. This robes them of courage
> and health, and instead of prayers from many, we hear the dread-
> ful national evil curses.

On the 20th, the women of the Muhlenberg household baked bread twice and distributed it and other food among the sick and feeble in the army. More fugitives from Philadelphia also claimed the hospitality of the minister.

Pastor Muhlenberg and his family were urged to flee as it was expected the vicinity of their home would become the scene of a battle. The Reverend Henry E. Muhlenberg, a son, and his wife and child, who were staying at Trappe, did conclude to continue their journey some miles farther, to New Hanover. Pastor Muhlenberg wanted his sick wife to accompany the son's family, but "she was not to be persuaded," says the journal, "but would rather live, suffer and die with me in Providence."

## The Battle of Germantown

From the Pottstown region, the American army moved toward Philadelphia by successive steps, for Washington was still determined to give battle again to the British if the opportunity offered. He was receiving reinforcements of militia from Pennsylvania and adjoining states, and he learned that Howe was sending some of his regiments to engage the American fortifications along the Delaware River below Philadelphia. The main body of the British army was encamped in Germantown, then a township in Philadelphia County, five miles north of the city of Philadelphia. Now Germantown is part of the city of Philadelphia. Early in October, Washington believed the time was at hand to attack the foe.

The British line extended east and west across Germantown, along Church Lane and School Lane, at right angles to the main street of the village at Market Square. From his camp at Worcester, twelve miles north of Germantown, Washington planned to move his army down four roads converging in Germantown, attacking the British at different points along their line. The main wing, under the command of Washington himself, was to proceed down Germantown road, the main street of Germantown. The left wing, with General Greene in command, would follow Limekiln road, which joined Church lane east of Germantown. Thus, Greene, it was hoped, might turn the British right flank. The Pennsylvania militia was to advance over Ridge Road, three miles west of Germantown Road, and keep the German troops in the left wing of the British line occupied so they could not come to the aid of the center.

As Greene was assigned to command the left wing, Muhlenberg, for the time, had charge of Greene's division in this wing.

The army, numbering about 9000 men, marched from its camp at Worcester after nightfall on October 3, and the battle opened at the upper end of Germantown at 5 A.M. the next day when the main wing, under Washington, encountered the British pickets at Mount Airy. Two regiments of British light infantry were posted along Germantown Road, one at the present Mount Pleasant Avenue and the other at Upsal Street, the latter being a mile in advance of the British main line. The Americans drove back the two regiments. Part of one of these regiments took possession of the house of Chief Justice Benjamin Chew, which the family had abandoned. The heavy stone walls of the house made it a veritable fortress, and the Americans sought in vain to dislodge the small band of redcoats that held it. Meanwhile, the troops of Wayne and Sullivan had proceeded farther down into Germantown, along both sides of the main street, and were fighting the two retreating regiments of the British in the backyards of Germantown homesteads.

Much depended upon the left wing of the American army under Greene. Its course over Limekiln Road carried it two miles to the east of Washington's command. Greene had more men than Washington. He, too, encountered a regiment of British light infantry, a mile in advance of the main line, and quickly compelled it to retreat. A heavy fog interfered greatly with plans for co-operation. One of the commands under Greene, that of General Adam Stephen, wandered far out of its course, moving westward until it collided with troops of Washington's wing. Subsequently, Stephen was tried and dismissed from the army for his misconduct in this battle.

The men under Muhlenberg acquitted themselves well. In their onrush, they proceeded into the settled part of Germantown, to the east of the main street, where they captured a battalion of British. The captors set up such a huzza that other British forces were attracted, and soon the Ninth Virginia Regiment, of Muhlenberg's brigade, commanded by Colonel George Matthews, found itself surrounded by the British and was compelled to surrender. The captive Virginians were immured in the

German Reformed Church at Market Square, and the prisoners held by the Americans were released.

Some of Muhlenberg's regiments engaged in bayonet fighting with the foe in the backyards and small farms of Germantown and Muhlenberg's horse was almost exhausted from repeatedly jumping over fences and stone walls. His troops had to come to his aid and pull down fences. Several times British sharpshooters made Muhlenberg their target, and bullets whistled close to him. Once he saw a young British officer seize the gun of a soldier and raise it to fire at Muhlenberg, but Muhlenberg quickly drew his revolver and shot the officer.

Meanwhile, Washington, halting at the Chew house and endeavoring in vain to dislodge the British that had converted it into a fort, heard nothing of Greene's progress on the east side. It was a principle of military science that a fortified place should not be permitted to remain in possession of the enemy in the rear. So, although part of his command had gone a half-mile beyond the Chew house into Germantown and Greene's men had penetrated Germantown on the east side, nevertheless, the commander-in-chief felt it expedient, after several hours' fighting, to order a retreat.

It was well he did so. Up to that time, the Americans had encountered only the advanced regiments of the British army. The main body of the foe was still down in the center of Germantown, a mile away. In response to the alarm, General Howe rode up into Germantown from his headquarters at Stenton, and soon he was bringing the trained regiments of his left wing into action, wheeling them in such a way as to threaten to entrap the Americans along Germantown Road.

The order to retreat came in time to enable the Americans to withdraw with slight loss and to carry off their wounded. On the east side of Muhlenberg's troops covered the retreat of Greene's wing and were the last to leave the field here, as at Brandywine.

Thus, after having marched all night and fought for four hours or longer, the tired troops retraced their steps to Worcester and then continued the retreat some miles farther, to the Perkiomen Valley, where Schwenksville now is.

Two days later Father Muhlenberg, at Trappe, wrote in his journal: "Yesterday the main American army had returned to about five miles from our house, to one side, where they buried their dead and fired a volley for each one, which we heard distinctly, as it lasted a long time."

For some time, Washington had hopes of inflicting a blow upon the British before going into winter quarters. The British soon abandoned their camp in Germantown and retired to Philadelphia. From the Perkiomen region, the Americans moved gradually toward Philadelphia, occupying camps in succession at Towamencin, Worcester, and Whitpain and remaining then in Whitemarsh for nearly six weeks.

So far as his father's journal shows, Peter Muhlenberg did not find it feasible to visit his parents at Trappe until October 18, though his brother Frederick had come to camp to see him. It was indeed a busy period for the American officers, for they had much to do in restoring their commands to the best possible status to meet any demands that Washington might require.

Coming to Trappe at noon on Saturday, October 18, General Muhlenberg brought news of the surrender of General Burgoyne's army to the Americans at Saratoga, which had been announced in the American army's camp at Worcester that morning. From Trappe, General Muhlenberg proceeded eight miles farther the same day to New Hanover, where brother Frederick acting as pastor of the Lutheran church at that place was staying.

In the interval between the Battle of Germantown and the winter camp at Valley Forge, General Muhlenberg was a member of two important courts-martial, one in which General Anthony Wayne was acquitted of any impropriety regarding the surprise of his command at Paoli in September, and the other wherein General Adam Stephen, of Virginia, was found guilty of inefficiency in the management of his troops at Germantown, the latter verdict resulting in Stephen's dismissal from the army.

## Whitemarsh and Valley Forge Camps

In the camp at Whitemarsh, Washington several times asked the general officers to give their opinions in writing on questions of the moment. Late in November, he submitted to them the desirability of making another attack upon the British. Muhlenberg was one of the four generals who favored such an attack.

The Americans remained on the defensive. Early in December, the British marched out of Philadelphia with the hope of overwhelming the Americans at Whitemarsh. After some skirmishing, Howe and his generals were convinced the Americans were too strongly posted to warrant a battle, and they withdrew into the city.

Another matter on which Washington sought the opinions of his generals was the site for the winter camp. Being a Pennsylvanian, no doubt General Muhlenberg's judgment was regarded as of special value. He did not favor close concentration but advised that the army be quartered in the territory between Reading and Lancaster or between Reading and Easton, huts being built for more robust soldiers, while the sick were placed in farmhouses. Thus, he believed the interior of Pennsylvania could be protected, and the distance of the army from the foe in Philadelphia would induce the latter to let the Americans alone in a period when inevitably their numbers would be greatly depleted.

Muhlenberg's suggestion was not adopted. Washington decided upon a closely concentrated camp at Valley Forge, a region which had not been specifically suggested by any of the generals.

It is an interesting question whether, if the army had been scattered over a wide extent of country, as Muhlenberg proposed, much of the sickness that swept through the winter camp at Valley Forge might have been avoided, and food might have been more readily obtained.

Early in December, Washington also asked the generals what they thought about the desirability of a winter campaign. While he had previously sanctioned the idea of another attack on the enemy, Muhlenberg felt that a winter campaign would be inadvisable and impractical, "at least if I am to judge of other brigades by my own, one single regiment of which has turned out ninety men unfit for duty on account of shoes and other necessaries." As winter advanced, he pointed out, sickness would increase, and it would be difficult to collect the militia. However, he did approve of making plans during the winter for a campaign to open early in the spring. He closed the letter with these characteristic words: "Should the question be decided otherwise, Your Excellency may be assured that any part entrusted to me shall be executed with the greatest cheerfulness." Such sentiments must have warmed the heart of Washington when information on the activities of the Conway Cabal came to his attention.

Most of the officers were against a winter campaign. On December 19, the army went into camp on the hills of Valley Forge, twenty-three miles northwest of Philadelphia, on the southern banks of the Schuylkill River. There, General Muhlenberg's brigade occupied the territory nearest the enemy, about the present village of Port Kennedy. This was a mile and a half distant from Washington's headquarters in the village of Valley Forge.

General Muhlenberg made his headquarters in the farmhouse of John Moore, along Trout Creek. John Moore, who owned 200 acres, died January 1, 1778, soon after the army came to the locality, and his widow, Jane, there-after lived in the house. The dwelling still stands though much altered.

Muhlenberg's brigade, constituting part of the front line of the camp, occupied the Moore farm and adjoining tracts. This region was not hilly woodland, like the country farther west where the greater part of the army was stationed. Most of the land was cultivated, though there also were some woods.

Upon arriving, the Virginians proceeded energetically to erect their huts, and it is said Muhlenberg's brigade completed the work of felling the trees and constructing the cabins in four days. Other commands on the hills required two weeks for this task.

A redoubt was built on John Moore's land and another on the adjoining farm of Mordecai Moore. Extensive lines of entrenchments, made by digging ditches and piling up the earth on the side toward the enemy, connected the redoubts and extended in front of the encampment, constituting the outer line of defense. The remains of the redoubts and trenches could be seen as late as the 1850s, though nothing is now visible of them.

After the huts had been built, General Muhlenberg seized an opportunity to cross the Schuylkill River and ride seven miles northward to the home of his parents in Trappe. Snow and rain were falling when he made his visit, on December 26—the "second Christmas" which was observed by the Germans as part of the great festival.

It was not a time of merrymaking for the Muhlenberg family. Threats had been made not only against Peter Muhlenberg but against his father. Sympathizers with the British cause were numerous in the neighborhood, and raiding parties of the British made occasional incursions into the rural districts, though they were not in the habit of penetrating as far as Trappe. However, it was rumored that the British, Hessians, and Tories all were bent upon capturing both the Lutheran pastor and his militant son and thus earning a handsome reward.

The father, while sympathizing with the American cause, had not been given to discussing political questions in the pulpit, and he had even been known to say some things of the American soldiers not at all complimentary to them, especially when they turned their horses into his buckwheat field or took possession of his church. As for the son Peter, the British would surely have been delighted to lay their hands on him, for in view of his having been a parson of the established Church of England, his treason was looked upon as especially heinous.

When Peter Muhlenberg made his Christmas visit to his parents, he found his mother in failing health. He wanted his parents to go to the Tulpehocken region in upper Berks County, where they would be secure from the disturbances occasioned by the movements of the opposing armies. Their daughter Eve Elizabeth was the wife of the Reverend Christopher Emanuel Schulze, who was the Lutheran pastor in the Tulpehocken region. The mother was satisfied to have her husband go, but she said she was too sick to undertake the journey. Naturally, the husband would not leave without his wife. So, wrote Pastor Muhlenberg in his journal, "we prayed jointly for advice to the good God and resolved in God's name to remain and await our destined fortune." They continued to dwell at Trappe throughout the time of the camp at Valley Forge and were not molested.

Whenever their son Peter came from the camp to see his parents, precautions were adopted to prevent his presence from becoming known in the neighborhood. At night, blankets were hung over the windows and doors. He never undressed, and his horse always remained saddled and close at hand. Once, it is said, he was pursued while returning to camp, but the fleetness of his horse saved him.

## His Loyalty Tested

To all the patriots in the army, the Valley Forge season was a time of trial and testing. To Peter Muhlenberg, it was a peculiarly critical period because of a controversy about seniority, a matter concerning which military men were always sensitive but which, at this time of irritability, was especially difficult.

In September 1776, Colonel William Woodford, commander of the Second Virginia Regiment, resigned his commission because, though he was the senior Virginia Colonel, Colonel Adam Stephen was promoted to brigadier general over his head. On February 21, 1777, when Muhlenberg was advanced to the rank of brigadier general, the same rank was also given to Colonels Weedon and Woodford, the latter having returned to the service. Woodford, though he had been out of the army for some time, now claimed to be senior brigadier general of the Virginia line because he had been that state's oldest colonel.

The question was not of much importance until the dismissal of Major General Stephen for misconduct at the battle of Germantown created a vacancy which it was thought might be filled by the appointment of the senior brigadier general from Virginia, Stephen being from that state.

To decide the question, a board of general officers met at Valley Forge March 2, 1778. By a majority of one vote, General Woodford was recognized as the senior officer, but because the vote was so close, the board agreed to refer the final decision to Congress.

General Muhlenberg had gone to his home in Woodstock to adjust his long-neglected private affairs, and while there, he learned of the question about seniority. He, therefore, hastened back to Valley Forge without accomplishing the object of his trip. It was then his firm purpose to resign his commission in the army.

A committee of Congress was in the camp, and Muhlenberg wrote to this committee setting forth his claim. In a letter to Washington a little later, he indicated that he was warranted in resigning if he were subjected to the humiliation of having Woodford recognized as his senior.

Officers were resigning right and left at that time, most of them because they received no adequate pay, and their families were in need.

Washington replied to Muhlenberg, April 10, in the following words:

> In answer to yours of this morning, I have only to say that the matter respecting your rank and that of Generals Woodford, Weedon, and Scott has been fully discussed several times by Congress, the committees of Congress, and a board of general officers, whose opinions all seemed to correspond.
>
> This contradicts the report that Congress was at all events determined to give preference to General Woodford, as it appears to me that their determination was founded upon the proceedings of the general officers. Their report was short because they had papers before them, which fully evinced that the respective claims had been duly considered, and there was, therefore, no need of recapitulating all that had passed. You know my opinion, which has been given in a conversation between us.
>
> I cannot judge of the feeling of others, but my own should generally be regulated by the opinions of a set of gentlemen who I conceive have been actuated by the purest principles of impartiality and justice, and I do not think that any officer will look upon submission to their decision as dishonorable. I would not be thought to press you to a hasty decision upon this matter; but

when you consider that we are upon the verge of the campaign, you will think with me that no time is to be lost; because if a successor should be necessary he will scarcely have time to be acquainted with the brigade before they are called to action.

No incident in his career so disproves the legend of a headstrong, impetuous Peter Muhlenberg, as does the outcome of this controversy about rank. Had he been the wild fire-eater of tradition, surely, he would have followed General Weedon's course and resigned. Instead, he remained at his post, accepting Washington's assurances that no dishonor was involved, which was supplemented by a resolution passed unanimously in Congress that the arrangement as to the Virginia generals "was founded upon principles not affecting the personal characters or comparative merits of those officers." General Weedon did not return to the service until 1780.

For a time, Muhlenberg was the only Virginia general on duty at Valley Forge. In May, he was commanding a division.

## Aids Christopher Sauer

At Valley Force General Muhlenberg further evidenced his greatheartedness when he interceded on behalf of Christopher Sauer, the German printer of Germantown, who had been taken into custody because he was suspected of sympathizing with the enemy.

In the same year that General Muhlenberg's father, the Reverend Henry Melchior Muhlenberg, had built Augustus Church at Trappe, 1743, the elder Christopher Sauer, in Germantown, printed his first American edition of the Bible in any European tongue. Sauer also published a newspaper that had a large circulation among the German settlers, and many religious books came from his press.

Christopher Sauer and Henry Melchior Muhlenberg represented opposite types of leadership. Muhlenberg had a mind open to progressive ideas. He was friendly with the clergy of the Anglican and Presbyterian churches. In the middle of the eighteenth century, when a group of leaders in Pennsylvania affairs organized the Society for the Propagation of Christian Knowledge Among the Germans of America, Pastor Muhlenberg gave his cordial support to the movement. On the other hand, Sauer represented the extremes of conservatism and opposed the school plan. This and other subjects afforded him occasion for attacks upon Pastor Muhlenberg in his paper.

The elder Sauer died, and his son of the same name continued the publishing house, attaining wealth. He was a minister of the Church of the Brethren or Dunkers, and because of his religious beliefs, he refused to subscribe to the declaration of allegiance to the American cause when the Revolution opened. Two of his sons identified themselves with the British, and the father made his home in Philadelphia during the winter of the British occupation of the city. Upon the evacuation of Philadelphia, the two sons departed with the British, but the father returned to his home in Germantown on May 22, 1778. Two nights later, a detachment of American troops surrounded the house and arrested Sauer. What followed he described in his journal in these words:

> It was a dark night. They led me through the Indian cornfields, where I could not come along as fast as they wanted me to go. They frequently struck me in the back with their bayonets till they brought me to Bastian Miller's barn, where they kept me till the next morning. Then they stripped me naked to the skin and gave me an old shirt and breeches much torn, then cut my beard and hair, and painted me with oil colors red and black, and so led me along barefooted and bareheaded on a very hot sunshiny day. * * * On the 26th at 9 o'clock, I arrived at the camp and was sent to the provo.
>
> My accusation in the mittimus was an oppressor of the righteous and a spy. On the 27th, in the morning, God moved the heart of the most generous General Muhlenberg to come to me and enquire into my affairs and promised that he would speak to General Washington and procure me a hearing, and the next

day sent me word that I should make a petition to George Washington, which I did; and through the good hand of Providence and the faithful assistance of the said General Muhlenberg, I was permitted to go out of the provo on the 29th of May.

Thus, the son of the Lutheran leader whom the elder Sauer had maligned came to the rescue of the younger Sauer when he was in dire distress. Subsequently, in proceedings instituted by the state of Pennsylvania, Sauer was called upon to stand trial on a charge of treason. He ignored the notification, in consequence of which all his property was confiscated and sold.

## Military Activities in 1778 and 1779

As spring approached, Washington asked his generals to give their opinions as to three choices: to remain in camp at Valley Forge, to attack the British in Philadelphia, or to move against New York. In his reply, Muhlenberg stated his conviction that continued inactivity would be fatal and that he favored transferring the scene of war to New York, where it would be easier to provision the army than in exhausted Pennsylvania and where the New England states would come to the aid of the army. By such a movement, the enemy would inevitably be driven to evacuate Philadelphia to protect New York.

News of the French alliance greatly stimulated the inclination for action. A council of officers convened on June 17, 1778, to consider the feasibility of attacking Philadelphia. The decision against such action was unanimous, but the following day the British evacuated Philadelphia, and the American army immediately set out from Valley Forge toward New Jersey in pursuit of the British on their march toward New York.

General Greene having been appointed quartermaster general, General Charles Lee now succeeded him as commander of the division consisting of the brigades of Muhlenberg and Scott. Thus, Muhlenberg once more was under the officer who had been his superior in the opening years of the war in the South. Greene, however, had stipulated that in battle, he should command his old division. Hence when the Americans encountered the British at Monmouth, New Jersey, on June 28, Muhlenberg's men were not in Lee's command when the retreat of that general moved Washington to a memorable outburst of wrath.

After the Battle of Monmouth, Muhlenberg's command, and indeed the entire army under Washington's immediate direction, took part in no further important engagement until the end of the war, in Virginia, three years later.

Washington concentrated his army at White Plains, New York, and all he could do with the ineffective troops and inadequate supplies available was to try to hold the Hudson Highlands as a center of strength for the Americans.

Raiding parties went out in search of supplies, and sometimes, clashes occurred between small forces of Americans and the British. While at White Plains, Muhlenberg commanded a body of picket troops that made reconnaissances in the direction of the enemy's lines. Later in the year, his brigade was one of those stationed at West Point.

When Washington sought the opinion of the generals, in October 1778, as to winter quarters, Muhlenberg again proposed, as he had the preceding year, that the army be scattered, instead of being concentrated and furthermore he urged that, with the example of the distress at Valley Forge in mind, the preparation of winter quarters should not be delayed until December. An arrangement such as Muhlenberg suggested was adopted, the army being quartered at different places in New York, New Jersey, and Connecticut.

Having been unable to conclude a satisfactory adjustment of his private affairs in Woodstock on his brief visit the preceding winter, Muhlenberg now applied to Washington, on October 22, for permission to go to Virginia for this purpose. He reminded Washington that when he hastened back from Virginia after that futile visit, he had expected to resign and thus be at liberty to look after his long-deferred personal problems, but as he had yielded to Washington's request to remain in the army, his own affairs were held in abeyance. Respecting his belongings in Woodstock, he wrote:

> I left my household furniture, stock, etc. in the glebe at Dun-
> more, which I rented for one year, from the 10th of January last,
> under the care of an overseer, who, I am informed is gone on the
> Indian expedition, and the vestry likewise notify me that they
> wish my effects removed to make room for a minister. As the en-
> emy have already broke me up in Philadelphia, I wish to save the
> little I have left in Virginia, as I could not in justice to my family
> continue in the service unless I knew them in some sort provided
> for. I do not, however, mean to ask permission to go so long as
> your Excellency shall think my services wanted.

Washington replied that both Woodford and Scott had gone to Virginia, and Muhlenberg was the only remaining Virginia general, and therefore, Washington hoped he would defer his visit. Thus, he remained with the army throughout the winter.

Muhlenberg's brigade, and that of Woodford, now constituted a division commanded by General Israel Putnam. As Putnam was often engaged elsewhere, Muhlenberg commanded the division during most of the winter.

This winter of 1778-9 passed much more comfortably than the pre-ceding one at Valley Forge. Sometimes Muhlenberg entertained in his headquarters at West Point, for he delighted in the company of congenial souls. One account mentions that on November 3, forty-one officers were his guests, and fourteen different dishes were on the table. After-ward, with General Putnam presiding, the guests responded to toasts, sang songs, listened to music, and wound up the evening with a dance.

At the end of November, the division under Muhlenberg was ordered from West Point to join the main contingent of the army at Middle-brook, New Jersey. Here also, he could indulge his spirit of hospitality. On New Year's Day, 1779, he gave a ball and supper, when, according to Dr. Thatcher, "not one of the company was permitted to retire until 3 o'clock in the morning."

The chief event of the ensuing summer of 1779 in which Muhlenberg's troops shared was the storming of Stony Point. From his base at New York, General Clinton, by a sudden dash up the Hudson Valley, captured the American posts at Stony Point and Verplank's Point. Washington planned to recapture Stony Point, an important stronghold along the Hudson. General Wayne was delegated to make the attack, with General Muhlenberg supporting him. The plan was successfully carried out on July 15. General Muhlenberg, with 300 men from his brigade, was stationed so they could either come to the aid of Wayne in the attack upon the British or else cover the retreat of the assailing force if it met with misfortune. Wayne executed the duty assigned him so effectively that the help of Muhlenberg's detachment was not needed.

With the army inactive most of the time, confusion resulted from desertions and lack of discipline, and Muhlenberg was much occupied trying to rectify affairs in his command.

## Takes Command in Virginia

The army spent the winter of 1779-80 near Morristown, New Jersey. As the British now were sending troops to the South, all the Virginia regiments with Washington were ordered to Charleston, South Carolina, in December 1779, and Muhlenberg was directed to take command of the American forces in Virginia. He spent some weeks in Philadelphia and arrived in Virginia in February 1780.

The two Carolinas, Georgia, and Virginia, now became the scene of the principal military operations of the Revolution. The British captured Charleston, South Carolina, and numerous conflicts occurred between small bodies of partisans. Conditions in many parts of the Carolinas were a little short of anarchy. Supporters of Great Britain organized many companies, and bitter internecine warfare resulted between them and the patriots.

Upon Virginia, the chief reliance had to be placed to keep the southern army supplied with men and food, for Virginia was then the richest and most populous of the thirteen states, and so far, it had suffered comparatively little from the war.

Muhlenberg first went to Richmond to collect men and munitions. But recruiting was at a low ebb, and prices of goods were at an astounding level. Muhlenberg himself had to pay $20,000 for a horse, the payment being in the greatly depreciated Continental currency. Even after Muhlenberg got together some troops, the state of Virginia had no money with which to pay them so that it was necessary to furlough them. Troops that remained could not parade for lack of clothes. The situation became worse in May 1780, when, by the capitulation of Charleston to the British, all the regular troops of Virginia became prisoners of war in the hands of the foe.

General Horatio Gates was now appointed to command a new American army in the South, and most of that army was to be raised in Virginia. Washington implored Muhlenberg to hasten to recruit. At Muhlenberg's suggestion, the Virginia Legislature on August 1 authorized a draft of 3000 men, though Muhlenberg had asked for 5000.

By September 1, 1780, Muhlenberg, at Chesterfield, Virginia, had several regiments filled. But they lacked clothing and arms. His letters to Congress in Philadelphia had brought no response, so he sent Colonel Christian Febiger to the capital to obtain the supplies needed. The Virginia recruits were forwarded to Gates at Hillsboro, North Carolina. Gates fought the Battle of Camden, in South Carolina, meeting a severe defeat.

Handicapped on every side, Muhlenberg nevertheless sought to provide the men so badly needed farther south to stem the advance of the British, under Lord Cornwallis, who now menaced Virginia itself. His desperate efforts in October brought down upon Muhlenberg the reproof of Gates, who objected because the men Muhlenberg sent him were without clothes, blankets, arms of accouterments, constituting "a naked rabble."

Now Clinton sent 3000 British troops from New York, under General Leslie, to Virginia. They arrived in the James River at Portsmouth on

October 15. Muhlenberg kept such troops as were at hand and set about assembling a new army for the defense of Virginia. The British raided the country along the James River. Militia assembled, and Muhlenberg took post fifteen miles from the enemy's lines. Having collected 5000 men, he advanced with them against Leslie's army and drove in the pickets. In November, the British boarded their ships and sailed back to New York, whereupon the Virginia militia was permitted to return home.

Meanwhile, General Greene had superseded Gates in command of the American forces in the South, and General von Steuben was sent to take command in Virginia. Von Steuben arrived on December 1, 1780, and assumed charge of the forwarding of troops to Greene's army, farther south. A court-martial of Gates was ordered, and Muhlenberg was appointed a member of the court. But the army officers were so much occupied about this time that the court never met, and Congress finally rescinded the order for the trial.

Von Steuben found himself in a dilemma, for while Greene was badly in need of reinforcements for the southern army, Governor Thomas Jefferson and the people of Virginia protested sending away more troops, believing their state was liable to a British invasion from the ocean. Another annoying feature was that so many American officers supposed to be on duty were at their homes or on jaunts about the state, notwithstanding Muhlenberg's orders had called on them to report to their commands.

When von Steuben, in December, directed a contingent of 400 men from Muhlenberg's command to join Greene in North Carolina, the officers signed a paper refusing to march because they had not been paid and food and proper clothing had not been provided. Muhlenberg, with Colonel Robert Hanson Harrison and Greene, induced the officers to withdraw the paper and march to North Carolina on December 14.

The British had not abandoned the idea of subduing Virginia. On January 2, 1781, a fleet arrived at Portsmouth with 2000 British troops under the command of General Benedict Arnold, through whose treason the year before the Americans had nearly lost West Point. Arnold took possession of Richmond, causing much damage there, but he soon retired down the James River.

Muhlenberg was in Woodstock on leave of absence. He had been home only three days when a messenger arrived from General von Steuben telling of the new invasion and asking him to take steps to protect northern Virginia. He set out immediately for Fredericksburg, and there began collecting the militia, which force, in response to further orders from von Steuben, he led on to the James River, taking a post with 800 infantry and some cavalry at Cabin Point. Von Steuben had his headquarters in Richmond, while Muhlenberg commanded in the field, instituting measures to check further raiding by Arnold.

A plan was proposed about this time to capture Arnold. Thomas Jefferson, governor of Virginia, wrote to Muhlenberg, urging the plan to be executed by "men from the western side of the mountains" —that is, men from Muhlenberg's Shenandoah Valley—who were known to Muhlenberg personally. If successful, a reward of 5000 guineas was promised to the party. There is reason to believe that an attempt was made to seize the traitor, but details of the undertaking were never revealed. Because just such a project was feared, Arnold was so carefully guarded that he could not be isolated and taken. According to one version, Colonel George Rogers Clark, a frontier hero, was chosen to direct the venture. A tradition of the incident tells that one of Clark's party was captured by the British and brought before Arnold. "What would be my fate if the Americans caught me?" asked Arnold. The reply was: "We would cut off that shortened leg wounded at Quebec and Saratoga and bury it with the honors of war, and then hang the rest of you."

A small French fleet appeared off Portsmouth, and Muhlenberg had high hopes the American army and the French navy would combine in an attack that would result in the taking of Arnold and his whole command. Muhlenberg now had about 2000 men. But the French ships refused to stay, the commander saying the Elizabeth River was too shallow for his ships. Muhlenberg implored him at least to remain where he was to prevent the escape of the British, but the French ships sailed away.

General Lafayette was now assigned to command the American army in Virginia, Washington realizing the likelihood of important developments there provided he could induce the French naval forces to lend their aid. Toward such co-operation, it was naturally expected that Lafayette's influence would count for much. Lafayette brought with him 1200 men from the Continental Army on the Hudson. Muhlenberg, meanwhile, kept Arnold confined in a narrow sector.

A curious British "joke" caused Muhlenberg some annoyance and anxiety now. He had sent 350 men, in command of Colonel Richard Parker, to attack a British post at Great Bridge. They captured the post and several British gunboats. On one of the boats, they found the baggage of Captain Stevenson, commander at Great Bridge. Examining this, the Americans came upon what seemed to be a letter written by Stevenson and addressed to General Isaac Gregory, commander of the North Carolina militia, stationed nearby. The letter discussed a plan for Gregory's surrender to Lieutenant Colonel John Graves Simcoe, of the British army. Parker turned the letter over to General Muhlenberg, who ordered the arrest of Gregory. Suspicion had prevailed for some time among the Americans that Benedict Arnold was not the only traitor in their ranks. Now it looked as though one had been caught. Simcoe heard of what had occurred, and he wrote to Colonel Parker declaring that the letter was only a joke and that there had been no negotiations between him and Gregory. Gregory was released, but because of the feeling aroused against him, he left the army.

While Arnold was in Virginia, General Muhlenberg received at least two letters from him. To the first letter, he did not reply, as is indicated by Arnold's second missive. Nor is there any record as to the outcome of the questions that Arnold raised. Arnold's second letter, dated Headquarters, Portsmouth, March 14, 1781, was as follows:

> I wrote you the 8th instant, by Lieutenant Herron, respecting the detention of a flag of truce, which left this place on the 1st of February, with my permission, to go to Westover, to which I beg leave to refer, and to which I have not received an answer. I have therefore sent Lieutenant Learmouth with a flag for an answer to my letter referred to, and expect, as you are a gentlemen, that an explicit and not an evasive answer will be returned to me. The violation of a flag of truce is so unprecedented among civilized,

nay among savage nations, and calls so loudly for redress or retaliation that I esteem it my duty to demand to know for what reasons mine has been violated in the instance of Lieutenant Hare, and that the vessel and people should be immediately released and returned to me. If I receive not a satisfactory answer or you persist to act in defiance of the law of nations, I shall be under the necessity of taking such measures, however disagreeable, and which I have hitherto avoided, as will teach a proper respect to flags of truce, and will convince those in power among you that I am not to be trifled with.

I beg you to remember that I have hitherto spared your defenseless towns and private property. I wish not to be forced into acts of severity at which the humane heart would recoil.

I beg leave also to observe (in compassion to your people prisoners with me) that I have either received none or evasive answers to every proposal I have made for an exchange of those unhappy people.

On March 19, 1781, Lafayette arrived in Muhlenberg's camp at Suffolk, twenty-six miles southwest of Norfolk, but he soon returned to his own troops, at the head of Chesapeake Bay, leaving Muhlenberg still in command of the forces opposing the British. A fleet brought 3000 men to reinforce Arnold, and it looked as though the purpose of the British was to form a junction with Lord Cornwallis' army in North Carolina. The Virginia militia who had served their term of three months insisted on going home. Muhlenberg, describing the situation, wrote that the militia "have partly discharged themselves and compelled me to discharge the remainder." One hundred deserted in one night. He was, therefore, under the necessity of retiring from the position he held close to the enemy's lines. He now had only 800 men, with but five rounds of cartridges. "So," he wrote in a letter, "nobody will be surprised if on the enemy's coming out I take myself out of his reach."

A large force of the British, under the command of General William Phillips and General Arnold, went up the James River in boats, debarking at City Point on April 24, 1781. General Muhlenberg placed his men, now numbering 1000, between the British and Richmond, and General von Steuben assumed command. An engagement continuing two hours ensued, sixty to seventy Americans being killed, while the British loss was trifling. The Americans retreated to Richmond.

Both in general orders and in his report to Congress, General von Steuben warmly praised Muhlenberg and his men for their stand against great odds, saying: "General Muhlenberg merits my particular acknowledgments for the good disposition which he made and the great gallantry with which he executed it."

Finally, on April 29, Lafayette and his detachment arrived, and Lafayette took command of operations in Virginia, while Muhlenberg, as a senior brigadier general, was assigned to the Continental troops that Lafayette had brought with him. Washington further reinforced Lafayette by sending to Virginia 900 men of the Pennsylvania line, under General Anthony Wayne.

Some of the harassing experiences which Muhlenberg encountered in trying to maintain discipline among the troops are suggested in a letter from him to General Washington on July 2, 1781, from Cumberland Old Court House, Virginia. He reported that eleven men had deserted, but "the most notorious villain of the whole" was apprehended, and after a court-martial was sentenced to be shot. He admitted deserting four times, stealing a horse, forging Muhlenberg's name to discharge papers, and a pass and joining the British. Nevertheless, Muhlenberg wrote he was "loath to order his execution until I could receive directions from your Excellency." However, other officers protested clemency or delay, and Muhlenberg, therefore, approved the sentence, and it was executed on July 16. Washington subsequently sanctioned all that had been done in the case.

## The Yorktown Campaign

The British general, Lord Cornwallis, after a series of misadventures in North Carolina, made his way with his army to Petersburg, Virginia, where he combined forces with Arnold on May 20, 1781. Southeastern Virginia was ravaged, the state government fleeing to Charlottesville. Cornwallis finally fixed upon Yorktown as his base of operations, and there he succeeded in bottling himself up so effectively that a splendid opportunity was offered to the Americans to win a decisive victory.

At New York, Washington, with his small Continental Army, continued to maneuver about the British in a way that caused Sir Henry Clinton, their commander, to hesitate about sending more men to Virginia. Nor were many new troops coming from England, for now, Great Britain was facing the united opposition of France, Spain, Holland, and the United States, and was carrying on widespread naval operations against these powers. So, Cornwallis was left to look after himself as best he could.

Washington sent word to Count DeGrasse, commander of a French fleet, then in the West Indies, urging him to bring his ships into the Chesapeake Bay. In his camp on the Hudson River, Washington continued his policy of keeping Clinton occupied. Suddenly on September 2, Washington and the Continentals, together with the French allies under Rochambeau, left the Hudson and proceeded on forced marches through New Jersey and Philadelphia to the head of Chesapeake Bay. Thence they were carried on French transports to the neighborhood of Yorktown.

Before the arrival of Washington, Lafayette feared Cornwallis might make a desperate effort to save himself by breaking through the American line and seeking refuge in North Carolina. To Wayne and Muhlenberg was given the duty of preventing such a move. Muhlenberg first concerned himself with getting out the North Carolina militia and destroying bridges, mills, and provisions. Then he posted his troops as close as possible to the British line at Yorktown, where the movements of the enemy could be kept under observation.

All the American brigades were pitifully weak. In the summer of 1781, Muhlenberg's brigade consisted of 800 men. By October it had been increased to 1000.

On September 14, Washington and Count Rochambeau, the latter commanding the French troops, were at Williamsburg, Virginia. Soon the combined armies began their advance upon Yorktown. The investment of the British lines was underway by the end of September, the purpose being to besiege the enemy and make gradual advances upon him.

The French and American forces totaled 16,600 men, about equally divided between the two nationalities. Cornwallis had about 8000 men.

Announcing the line of battle in general orders on September 27, Washington placed the brigades of Muhlenberg and Moses Hazen on the right of the front line, under the command of Lafayette, and Muhlenberg's brigade, preceded by Colonel William Lewis' Corps of Riflemen, was to constitute the advanced guard.

The siege continued without conflicts until the night of October 15, when two flank redoubts of the British were stormed and captured with the bayonet. The attack on one redoubt was made by a French detachment. Two brigades of Americans under the command of Muhlenberg captured the other redoubt.

Many accounts say Colonel Alexander Hamilton led the American storming party on this occasion. It has been shown, however, that, while Colonel Hamilton commanded a regiment in the attack and acquitted himself with heroism, the movement was in charge of Muhlenberg as commander of the two brigades.

After attaining the interior of the redoubt, Muhlenberg was slightly injured, and hence Hamilton wrote the report of the movement, which caused credit to be given him as commander. It was characteristic of Muhlenberg that he did not enter into the controversy about the matter subsequently.

An obituary article in the *Aurora*, Philadelphia, at the time of General Muhlenberg's death asserted he led the storming party at Yorktown and "displayed the hero, the human man, and gave a luster to the name of American by blending valor and intrepidity with magnanimity—having entered the breach and every man of his party, himself included, wounded, he nobly stayed the hand of his fellow-citizens from the exercise of the lawful rights of war; he stormed, conquered and spared the vanquished."

One of his aides who survived until 1840 was quoted as declaring that General Muhlenberg led the storming party in person.

By the loss of the flank redoubts, Cornwallis was convinced his position was no longer tenable. A parley between the opposing forces took place on October 17, culminating in the surrender of the British army two days later.

Muhlenberg suffered from ill-health now. On October 23, he wrote to Washington from Williamsburg, saying he had been afflicted with a violent fever for ten days and asking that he be permitted to go to his home in Woodstock. Since he had entered the service, he had been able to spend but three days in Woodstock. The permission sought was granted, and General Muhlenberg remained with his family in the Shenandoah Valley until the following spring.

## Final Scenes of the War

Cornwallis' surrender at Yorktown virtually ended the war. But that fact was not then evident. The British still held such important centers as New York, Charleston, and Savannah. The Americans were exhausted, both in manpower and finances. Only with strong French aid had Yorktown been won. How long such aid might continue was uncertain. On the other hand, England also was keenly feeling the losses of the long war against three great European nations, and the Whigs in England urged that the American war be abandoned to concentrate effort on the conflict elsewhere. The latter policy eventually prevailed. But Washington and the other American leaders could not forecast such action in 1781. Hence the only safe course for them was to maintain the army at the best strength possible.

Rochambeau's French troops remained in Virginia during the winter of 1781-2, but in 1782 they moved to the north. It was then necessary to begin recruiting in Virginia. To such service, General Muhlenberg was assigned in the spring of 1782, and the troops he assembled were forwarded to General Greene's army in South Carolina. From his rendezvous at Cumberland Old Court House, he continued to send troops to the army until the British evacuation of Charleston made it unnecessary to continue military activities in the South.

Thereafter, General Muhlenberg's headquarters were in the barracks in Winchester, at the foot of the Shenandoah Valley. Here he was only thirty miles from his family in Woodstock, and could frequently visit them. It is said he sometimes married couples. Recruiting continued until March 1783, when news arrived of the signing of the preliminaries for peace. Muhlenberg's duties then involved the disbanding of troops in the service in Virginia, his jurisdiction including Fort Pitt, where Pittsburgh now is, in western Pennsylvania.

On September 30, 1783, Congress promoted General Muhlenberg to the rank of major general. The disbanding of the army was ordered the following November. The same year Muhlenberg became one of the original members of the Order of the Cincinnati.

## Muhlenberg Memorials at Woodstock

On returning to Woodstock, Muhlenberg met the suggestion that he resume the ministry with the comment that "it would never do to mount the parson after the soldier." By this time, the name of the county of which Woodstock was the seat of government had been changed from Dunmore to Shenandoah, for the royal governor of Virginia whose name had been adopted when the county was created had completely discredited himself through his aggressions in the early years of the war.

In November 1783, General Muhlenberg removed his family from Woodstock to the home of his parents, in Trappe, Pennsylvania.

The Woodstock church, where Muhlenberg had preached his thrilling farewell sermon in 1776, was abandoned after the war. The formerly established church of Virginia could now no longer claim governmental support through taxation. Moreover, most of its ministers were in disfavor for having supported the cause of the crown. For many years the life of the average parson in Virginia had been far from exemplary. They were not of a type of character to cope with difficulties, and when their livings were taken from them, they yielded to the stress of conditions, and the churches were abandoned and the glebe lands sold. Not until after the Reverend William Meade became bishop of Virginia, in 1829, was the Episcopal church revived in that state.

The German Lutherans of the Shenandoah Valley took steps to effect congregational organization independent of the old influences of the established church, and the Reverend Christian Streit, who had been chaplain of the German Regiment in the early days of the war, became pastor of a Lutheran congregation in Winchester in 1785. About 1790, the Reverend Paul Henkel assumed the Lutheran pastorate in New Market, south of Woodstock, also ministering to the Lutherans of Woodstock. The church in which Peter Muhlenberg preached stood on the borders of the square in Woodstock until 1848, though not regularly used by any congregation. In 1803, a Lutheran congregation was organized in Woodstock, building its church in a different part of the town from that where the old church stood. This congregation still exists and has a large membership.

An Episcopal parish was founded in Woodstock in 1882. Its membership was small, but it built its church close to the site of Muhlenberg's old church on the Square, and it claims to be the legitimate successor of the original Beckford Parish. A sign in front of the church reads: "Emmanuel Episcopal Church, Beckford Parish. Open daily for prayer and meditation. Sunday service, summer, 8 P.M., winter, 7:30 P.M. General Peter Muhlenberg was the first rector of this church."

A large window in the church is inscribed thus: "In memory of General Peter Muhlenberg, of Revolutionary fame, the first rector to officiate in the first Episcopal church built in Beckford Parish, in the Colony of Virginia, upon the site of which this church stands."

The Lutheran church in Woodstock also is named Emanuel—with one "m."

A pewter communion set and an altar cloth used in the Woodstock church when Peter Muhlenberg was the pastor have been preserved in Woodstock. Upon the altar cloth, the following is embroidered:

*Frederich Hengerer*
*Eva Maragreda Hengerin*
*Wutstack*
*Gott allein die Her*
*1767*

In 1930, the people of Woodstock placed a bronze tablet upon the front wall of their ancient courthouse, on the Square, commemorating both the building of the courthouse, in 1791, and Peter Muhlenberg's sermon in the church on the opposite side of the square, in 1776.

John Murray, Earl of Dunmore

Raleigh Tavern, Williamsburg, Virginia

Carpenters' Hall, Philadelphia,
Pennsylvania

Peyton Randolph

Saint John's Church, Richmond, Virginia

Patrick Henry

Thomas Jefferson

George Washington

Painting depicting "The Muhlenberg Myth" sermon

Thomas Buchanan Read

The Reverend Christian Streit

British General Henry Clinton

General Charles Lee

Battle of Sullivan's Island

General George Weedon

Major General Nathanael Greene

British General William Howe

British Admiral Richard Howe

British General John Burgoyne

Falls of the Schuylkill, Pennsylvania

Marquis de Lafayette

General Pulaski

General Charles Scott

Stenton, the home of the Logans, in Philadelphia, Pennsylvania

British General Lord Cornwallis

Birmingham Friends' Meeting House

Battle of Brandywine

Washington's field tent

Battle of Germantown

Washington reviewing the troops arriving at Valley Forge, Pennsylvania

The farmhouse of John Moore, along Trout Creek, near Valley Forge, Pennsylvania

General William Woodford

Battle of Monmouth

General Israel Putnam

Battle of Stony Point

General Horatio Gates

General Baron von Steuben

British General Benedict Arnold

Colonel George Rogers Clark

Count Rochambeau

Battle of Yorktown, assault on Redoubt 10

Reverend Paul Henkel

Emmanuel Church, Woodstock, Virginia

Peter Muhlenberg's communion items from Woodstock, Virginia

# IV

## POLITICAL AND CIVIC CAREER

### A Journey to the Wilds of Kentucky

Returning to Pennsylvania after the close of the Revolution, General Muhlenberg at first contemplated entering the trade in Philadelphia with a brother-in-law who was a merchant. His earliest inclinations, it will be recalled, were toward a business career. But the Philadelphia project did not develop satisfactorily and was abandoned. Then General Muhlenberg considered settling in Ohio on lands to which he was entitled due to his military service. His quota of such lands totaled 13,000 acres.

About this time, he was appointed to direct the distribution of the bounty lands which the state of Virginia had granted to the soldiers from that state for service in the Revolutionary War. These grants were mostly in Virginia's western domain, in the Ohio Valley, in the territory later comprised within the states of Ohio and Kentucky. Muhlenberg's official duties required him to go to the Falls of the Ohio River, now Louisville, Kentucky. So, he decided to make the journey to Ohio and Kentucky both in his own interests and as the authorized representative of Virginia. He also took with him commissions to locate lands awarded to General von Steuben and other officers of the Revolutionary army.

A journal that General Muhlenberg kept during his travels has been preserved, and it presents a vivid picture of the difficulties incidental to the undertaking. Riding on horseback, he was on the way from February 22, 1784, until April 11. Today an automobile makes the same trip in a day.

His brother, Frederick A., accompanied him from Trappe through Falkner Swamp to the house of Francis Swaine, their brother-in-law, in Berks County, where they remained overnight. The next day, Frederick returned to Trappe, while the general bought equipment for his journey.

On February 24, he arrived in Reading, staying for a day with relatives. From the 26th until the 28th, he was at the house of another brother-in-law, the Reverend Christopher E. Schulze, at Tulpehocken.

Progress was difficult because of intense cold and deep snow. On March 2, he crossed the Susquehanna on the ice at Harris' Ferry, now Harrisburg. At Carlisle, there was another short halt, and in the evening, General Muhlenberg witnessed a performance of *The Douglas Tragedy*, given in the old military barracks by students of the recently established Dickinson College. "The whole performance was as well as could be expected," he noted, for evidently, this was not the first time he had endured student theatricals. Here Captain Frederick Paschke, a Pennsylvania officer in the Revolution, joined Muhlenberg and accompanied him throughout the journey.

Continuing through Shippensburg, the passage over the Allegheny Mountains was eased somewhat, for, although more than two feet of snow covered the primitive road, yet a path was broken for Muhlenberg and his companion by forty pack horses that preceded them.

Describing his own appearance on the trail, he noted when he was at Bedford, on March 6, that he resembled Robinson Crusoe— "four belts around me, two braces of pistols, a sword and rifle slung, besides my pouch and tobacco pipe, which is not a small one." Exposure had so tanned his face that the natives mistook him for a Spaniard. As no one recognized him, he sometimes sat in taverns and listened to loungers retelling war reminiscences and discussing politics, and occasionally he heard his own name mentioned, "sometimes in one way and sometimes in another."

When the travelers arrived at Fort Pitt, now Pittsburgh, on March 10, the ice was breaking up in the rivers. Thence the journey was to be made in boats on the Ohio River, but snowstorms and other adverse weather conditions delayed departure until March 31.

Muhlenberg joined fortunes with other travelers in a fleet of five boats. One of the boats was named for Muhlenberg. Another the facetious voyagers dubbed *The Carpenter's Mistake.*

On both sides of the river was a wilderness. Rumors told of hostile natives lurking in the vicinity. Frequent stops were made to permit hunting ashore. On April 5, a buffalo and a deer were killed in Ohio, at the mouth of the Scioto River, at present-day Portsmouth, Ohio. Later three more buffaloes were shot near the Little Miami River, but they were so lean that the hunters decided to kill no more of these animals. All the game was in poor condition as the result of a severe winter, and many dead animals were seen in the woods.

Two of the travelers who went ashore on April 9 were lost. After a futile search for them, three others were left behind to continue inquiries, while the remainder of the party proceeded down the river. On the evening of the 10th, they discovered the missing men on the shore of the river.

The destination was the Falls of the Ohio River, now Louisville, Kentucky. Arriving there on April 11, they were greeted with a salute from Fort Nelson. Besides the fort, the town consisted of a courthouse, prison, and seven cabins.

On April 22 and 23, General Muhlenberg conducted a lottery to establish the order of choice among the land claimants. As the Indians were disposed to resent the intrusion of the settlers, Muhlenberg called on the county lieutenant to provide a militia guard to permit the locating and surveying of the land for the Virginia war veterans. No militia responded. Then an effort was made to organize a guard of fifty men to serve for $45 a month. This also failed. Consequently, the survey was postponed until a more favorable time.

The land to which General Muhlenberg himself was entitled, he located in Ohio, on the banks of the Scioto River. Of this, he traded 1000 acres for a like tract in Kentucky, nine miles from the Falls of Ohio, and he also joined a syndicate in the purchase of 200,000 acres in Kentucky.

As nothing further could be accomplished now in the distribution of the veterans' lands, General Muhlenberg returned home, accompanying a party across Kentucky to the Cumberland River and proceeding thence through North Carolina and Virginia. While crossing Kentucky, few settlements were encountered. At night the party would encamp and post guards for fear of natives. Thus, it fell to the lot of the former general to take his turn as sergeant of the guard.

The most important Kentucky settlement through which they passed was Harrod's Station, later Harrodsburg. In that locality, Muhlenberg visited one of the pioneer settlers, Colonel Abraham Bowman, who had been lieutenant colonel of Muhlenberg's old German Regiment. Here Muhlenberg was stricken with fever and ague. His own party having proceeded, Muhlenberg, on recovering, joined another group of travelers numbering forty-six. He noted that they traversed 120 miles before seeing another cabin.

Coming into Virginia, he spent a few days in Staunton and Woodstock in the Shenandoah Valley, and on June 25, he was once more at his home in Trappe.

Having learned on his trip of the dissatisfied attitude of the Indians in the Ohio River Valley, General Muhlenberg wrote to Governor Thomas Mifflin, of Pennsylvania, on this subject and urged that steps be taken to pacify the natives and negotiate a treaty with them so the settlement of the Ohio country might be undertaken. Otherwise, he feared an Indian war would break out on the frontier.

He looked forward to making his home on his western lands, and he arranged to go again to the Ohio region the following September. He spent the winter of 1784-5 in Ohio and Kentucky, located additional military grants, including those of General von Steuben, and completed his duties as superintendent on behalf of Virginia. In the spring of 1785, he returned to his Pennsylvania home.

So great was the terror among settlers in the Ohio Valley lest the extensive appropriation of land by Virginia for military bounties should inspire the Indians to wage a war of extermination against the pioneers, that representations to this effect were made to the Virginia Legislature, and in October 1784, the Legislature authorized the government of the state to suspend the surveys of military lands for as long a period as he might deem necessary. By proclamation, the governor designated the term of suspension to continue until January 10, 1786. When that time arrived, the federal government, now in control of the western lands, renewed the order against the surveys. The Indian title was not extinguished until 1818, and after that, Kentucky would not permit the locating of military warrants in that state. While many of Virginia's Revolutionary soldiers were prompt to claim the lands allotted and became settlers in Ohio, Kentucky, and Tennessee, nevertheless, thousands who delayed until after the cessation of surveys did not obtain grants in this region. To satisfy these claimants, Congress set apart large tracts of other western lands.

## In Pennsylvania's Executive Council

In the journal of his first western journey, General Muhlenberg wrote of overhearing political discussions in which his name was mentioned, the participants in the discussion, not knowing the man about whom they talked was present. As a Revolutionary soldier with an unblemished reputation and a man who was popular among the German settlers, General Muhlenberg could not escape political considerations. Already his younger brother, Frederick A., also bred to the ministry, had entered upon a political career. He had continued preaching some years after Peter entered the army, assisting his father in Pennsylvania churches, but in 1779, he abandoned the ministry when he was elected to the Continental Congress. The following year he became a member of the State Assembly and was chosen its speaker. When his brother Peter returned home, Frederick A. was a member of the Pennsylvania Board of Censors and a justice of the peace. Montgomery County was created in 1784 from the western part of Philadelphia County. It included Trappe, where the Muhlenbergs lived. The court of the new county consisted of the justices of the peace in the county, and Frederick A. Muhlenberg was president judge. He was also appointed register of wills and recorder of deeds of the new county.

General Muhlenberg's entrance into politics was in the capacity of a member of the Supreme Executive Council of Pennsylvania. Under the state constitution adopted in 1776, this body was the executive power of the state, there being no governor. The Council consisted of twelve elected members, one from each county and one from the city of Philadelphia. One-third of their number went out of office yearly, and after serving three years, no member was eligible for re-election until four more years elapsed.

At the election on October 11, 1785, General Muhlenberg was chosen to represent the new county of Montgomery in the Council. He was unopposed, and 578 votes were cast for him in the three election districts of the county.

When the Council organized, in Philadelphia, on October 18, General Muhlenberg was not present, nor did he appear to attend the daily meetings of the Council until November 2. After that, he missed only a few sessions. Benjamin Franklin, who had returned to Philadelphia from Europe a short time before and had been elected the councilor from the city of Philadelphia, was chosen to preside over the Council.

In the Council, General Muhlenberg was again called upon to aid in allotting lands to Revolutionary soldiers. This time these "donation lands," as they were called, were the gift of the state of Pennsylvania to the men from that state who were enrolled in the Continental Army. The Assembly, by an act of 1780, had promised to award such a "donation," and by a further act of 1783 the lands so to be bestowed were in western Pennsylvania, comprising all of Mercer and Crawford Counties, nearly all of Erie and parts of Lawrence, Butler, Armstrong, Venango, Forest, and Warren Counties. This region was then wild and unsettled. Tracts ranging in size from 200 to 500 acres were listed in series according to the suitability of the soil for farming. It was thought to assure fairness in the distribution by requiring all applicants to appear in person on stipulated days and draw tickets from a lottery wheel. A committee of the Supreme Executive Council, the act directed, was to supervise the lottery. General Muhlenberg was appointed on this committee in October 1786, together with John Boyd, Jonathan Hoge, Stephen Balliet, William Brown, and Samuel Dean. General William Irvine was named as agent to explore the lands and see that the assignments according to the lottery were properly put into effect. However, the complicated procedure that had been devised proved impracticable, and later radical changes were made in the method of distribution. Allotments of "donated lands" continued until the second decade of the nineteenth century.

At the reorganization of the Supreme Executive Council, October 31, 1787, Franklin was retained as president and General Muhlenberg was elected vice president. The election and installation of the officers was a ceremonious occasion. The Council and Assembly met in joint session, and after the choice of the president and the vice president, proclamation thereof was made. A procession was formed, led by constables with staves, sub-sheriffs with wands, the high sheriff, and the coroners with wands. Then followed the judges of all the courts, state, admiralty, and county; different court officers; state and national officers; "his excellency the president and the honorable the vice president"; the members of the Council two and two; the speaker and members of Assembly; the door-keepers and sergeants-at-arms; the provost and faculty of the University; militia officers and citizens. When all were in their assigned places, the oath of office was administered to the president and vice president.

Franklin, now 81 years old, attended few sessions of the Council during the following year, so that it fell to the lot of General Muhlenberg to fulfill the functions of chief executive of the state, presiding at meetings of the Council, directing the carrying out of its orders and conducting an extensive correspondence in its behalf.

The most important matter that required his attention was the controversy in the Wyoming region due to the conflicting claims of Pennsylvania and Connecticut. Pennsylvania officials who went there to adjust land claims were mobbed and imprisoned. Congress finally sent troops into the Wyoming Valley, and the disorders were subdued. Before he was elected vice president, the State Assembly in March 1787 had appointed General Muhlenberg as a commissioner, along with Timothy Pickering and Joseph Montgomery, to settle the disputes arising from the grants made by Connecticut, but he resigned from the commission before it began its work.

About this time occurred the death of General Muhlenberg's father, the venerated Reverend Henry Melchior Muhlenberg. He breathed his last at his home in Trappe on Sunday morning, October 7, 1787, being buried three days later alongside the church where he had so often preached.

Both General Muhlenberg and his brother, Frederick A., lent their powerful support to bring about the ratification in Pennsylvania of the new federal Constitution formulated in 1787. Frederick A. Muhlenberg presided over the state convention, which accepted the Constitution.

Philadelphia arranged for a big celebration as soon as it should become known that the requisite number of states had ratified the Constitution. On June 21, 1788, word arrived that New Hampshire, the ninth state, had given its consent. Accordingly, plans were made for the demonstration of July 4. Before that date, a tenth state, Virginia, also approved the Constitution. In the procession, comprising military bodies, civic societies, trades, and professions, General Muhlenberg headed the eleventh division, designated in honor of "the convention of the states." He rode on horseback and carried a blue flag on which could be read in silver letters, "Seventeenth of September 1787," that being the date of the adoption of the Constitution in the convention called to prepare it.

An act of the Pennsylvania Assembly, in 1787, incorporating the German College and Charity School of Lancaster, Pennsylvania, designated General Muhlenberg as one of the trustees. His brother, the Reverend Henry E. Muhlenberg, then pastor of Trinity Lutheran Church, Lancaster, became principal of the new school, which was later known as Franklin College, the predecessor of Franklin and Marshall College.

## Elected to Congress

In the first election for members of the House of Representatives of the United States under the new Constitution, in 1788, Pennsylvania's eight members were chosen on one state-wide ticket. Two of those elected were

General Peter Muhlenberg and Frederick A. Muhlenberg, who, however, were candidates on opposing tickets.

The Federalists made nominations at a convention held in Lancaster on November 3, 1788. The convention was composed of two delegates from each county in the state and a like number from the city of Philadelphia. The following candidates for members of the Federal House of Representatives were chosen: Thomas Hartley, York County; Henry Wynkoop, Bucks; Stephen Chambers, John Allison, George Clymer, Philadelphia; Thomas Scott, Washington; Thomas Fitzsimmons, city of Philadelphia, and Frederick A. Muhlenberg, Montgomery.

The Anti-Federalists, later known as Democratic-Republicans or Republicans, and finally as Democrats, met in Harrisburg and nominated these candidates: General Peter Muhlenberg, Daniel Hiester, William Findley, Charles Pettit, General William Irvine, William Montgomery, Blair McClenachan, and Robert Whitehill.

It was asserted by the Federalists that four of the Harrisburg nominees, including General Muhlenberg, were not Anti-Federalists, but since they supported the recently adopted federal constitution, they could properly be classed as Federalists.

The election took place on November 26. More than a week elapsed before the returns from all the counties were received and counted. Then it was seen that six members of the Lancaster ticket and two of the Harrisburg ticket had been elected, the two on the latter ticket being General Muhlenberg and Daniel Hiester, of Berks County, both of whom were popular among the German settlers and polled a large vote in the German counties. The Federalists declined to attribute their election to Anti-Federal sentiment among the voters.

The victorious candidates on the Lancaster ticket were Messrs. Clymer, Fitzsimmons, Hartley, Scott, and Wynkoop, besides Frederick A. Muhlenberg.

The total votes cast for the congressional candidates throughout the state were as follows, showing that the two Muhlenberg brothers led their respective tickets: F. A. Muhlenberg, 8707; Wynkoop, 8246; Hartley,

8163; Clymer, 8094; Fitzsimmons, 8086; Scott, 8068; Peter Muhlenberg, 7417; Hiester, 7403; Allison, 7067; Chambers, 7050; Findley, 6586; Irvine, 6492; Pettit, 6481; Montgomery, 6348; McClenachan, 6223; Whitehill, 5850.

Shortly prior to his election to Congress, General Muhlenberg's three-year term in the Supreme Executive Council of Pennsylvania expired. The last session of the Council he attended was on October 13, 1788, when an order was granted for the salary due him to that date. Benjamin Franklin presided when the Council met the following day. Then it was discovered that Muhlenberg had not formally resigned his office of vice president, though he had left the city. The Council hastily sent a messenger after him with the request that he forward his resignation by the messenger. The Council met again that evening in Franklin's house when the messenger produced General Muhlenberg's resignation, and it was accepted, David Redick being elected vice president.

General Muhlenberg and his brother, Frederick A., left Philadelphia March 2, 1789, for New York, the capital of the nation, where Congress was to organize on March 4. They took up their abode in Chatham Row with their brother-in-law and sister, the Reverend Dr. John Christopher Kunze, and his wife, Margaret Henrietta Muhlenberg. Dr. Kunze was the leading Lutheran pastor in New York at the time and professor of oriental languages at Columbia College.

The old New York City Hall, Wall Street, at the head of Broad Street, erected in the 1700s, had been reconstructed for the occupancy of Congress, under the direction of Major Charles L'Enfant, a French engineer, and architect, citizens of the city having subscribed the funds necessary to meet the expense. It was now called Federal Hall.

When March 4 came, only eight senators and thirteen representatives were present; hence organization had to be postponed awaiting the appearance of a quorum. The House assembled on April 1 and the Senate five days later.

Frederick A. Muhlenberg was elected Speaker of the House, and he was escorted to his post of duty by cavalry and a procession of citizens.

General Muhlenberg was appointed a member of the committees on national defense, regulation and discipline of the militia, and the reserved military bounty lands of Virginia.

The first business was to count the electoral vote for President and then send Charles Thomson, secretary of the old Continental Congress, to Mount Vernon to notify Washington of his election. Weeks elapsed before Washington arrived in New York, and finally, he was inaugurated on April 30.

Many grave problems confronted the First Congress, including action on amendments to the Constitution to correct defects that had come to light. But the printed proceedings of the sessions of the House do not show that General Muhlenberg ever made a speech, either in the First Congress or in the later congresses of which he was a member. Nor was he given to speechmaking outside Congress, notwithstanding he was active in politics and public affairs to the end of his life. This reticence is even more striking when it is remembered that he was trained for preaching, and even though no longer occupying the pulpit, he might readily have been excused for continuing a hortatory tenor of public admonition. Perhaps his ministerial career had taught him the truth of the Biblical allusion to the tongue as an unruly member. At any rate, his disinclination to indulge in oratory in an age when oratory flourished tends further to discredit the legends of his impetuosity and fiery flourish.

In this Congress, one of the unprecedented questions awaiting resolution was that of the President's title. Though the new nation was a republic, still many of those engaged in establishing the government believed the office of chief magistrate should be hedged about with considerable dignity, and the President should be distinguished by some rhetorically pleasing salutation, such as His Excellency or His Highness. Muhlenberg was averse to such notions, and his aversion cast a cloud for a time upon the relations between himself and Washington. The story, as afterward told, evidently upon Muhlenberg's own authority, was in this wise:

Washington was said to have favored the title of "High Mightiness," such as was applied to the Stadholder of Holland. The matter was before committees of both houses, when Muhlenberg, with several other representatives, was a guest of Washington at dinner. The title became a subject of discussion, and Washington asked:

> "General Muhlenberg, what do you think of the title of 'High Mightiness'?"
>
> One of those at the table was Henry Wynkoop, a Pennsylvania representative of large stature.
>
> Muhlenberg, replying to Washington, said: "Why, General, if we were certain the office would always be held by men as large as yourself or my friend, Mr. Wynkoop, it would be appropriate enough; but if a President as small as my opposite neighbor should be elected it would become ridiculous."

Washington's diary shows that General Muhlenberg dined with the President on January 7, March 11, and May 6, 1790. When the matter of the presidential title came to a vote, Muhlenberg voted with the majority against any kind of title. Washington was displeased, it is said. Soon thereafter, it was necessary to send an army against hostile Indians in the region north of the Ohio River. Muhlenberg had become familiar with conditions there on his two western trips, and because of his experience in the Revolution, he was proposed for the command of the army. However, the little clash over the presidential title, according to gossip of the times, impelled Washington to overlook Muhlenberg and appoint General Arthur Saint Clair to the command. Saint Clair had been made governor of the Northwest Territory the preceding year. Eventually, because he proved his inadequacy, it was necessary to assign the military command in the Northwest Territory to others.

The First Congress was called upon to determine the permanent location of the federal capital. Pennsylvania laid claim to the capital because that state was about in the middle of the chain of states stretching along the Atlantic seaboard, which then constituted the nation. But Pennsylvania's two senators were divided on the question, Robert Morris favoring the banks of the Delaware River, opposite Trenton, where Morrisville later came into existence, while William Maclay proposed the Susquehanna Valley as most suitable. General Muhlenberg voted for the latter site. However, through a coalition of New York with the southern states, the District of Columbia, on the Potomac, was chosen.

General Muhlenberg interested himself in obtaining from Congress an annuity for General von Steuben, to compensate him for relinquishing offices and opportunities in Germany to join the American army in the Revolution. A grant of $2500 a year was made to von Steuben.

## Pennsylvania Politics

Pennsylvania was now agitating the revision of its constitution, adopted in 1776. Numerous defects in that code had come to attention. Chiefly was it thought desirable to abandon the one-chamber Legislature and follow the precedent of the national Congress by having a senate and a house of representatives. A new constitution was formulated and placed before the voters of the state in 1790. General Muhlenberg supported it, and his influence among the Germans was powerful in bringing about its adoption.

In colonial times, the Germans of Pennsylvania often sided with the Quakers in opposition to the proprietaries, and through the help of the Germans, the Quakers maintained control of the government long after they had ceased to have a numerical majority of the population. Even before the Revolution, the Quakers were no longer potent in governmental affairs, and when their pacifist attitude caused them to be classed with the Tories, they lost virtually all political power in the state. The Germans were now a powerful political factor in their own strength.

In the early 1790s, the factional lines in the politics of the state were drawn upon the question of support or opposition to the federal or state constitution. Gradually the cleavage of political ideas developed upon the nature of the federal government, the followers of Washington and

Hamilton supporting a strong central government, while those who looked to Thomas Jefferson for their political doctrines insisted upon wide power for the states and the people. The former became known as Federalists and the latter as Anti-Federalists, Democratic-Republicans or Republicans, and later as Democrats.

General Muhlenberg, throughout his political career, was an adherent of Thomas Jefferson, and his influence was exerted on behalf of Jefferson's party, which after a few years, became dominant in Pennsylvania. However, he did not follow the Jeffersonians in all their extremes in their theories of government by the masses, especially as exemplified in the French Revolution.

Writing in 1805 to Joseph Hiester, also a follower of Jefferson, Muhlenberg expressed his disapproval of ultra-democratic tenets which were being preached in Pennsylvania in these words:

> That many wish to fish in troubled waters is evident; and that
> some have reached the height of impudence and are lost to all
> sense of shame is certain. For heaven's sake, only read that shame-
> less toast, drank publicly on the Fourth of July last— "The equal
> distribution of property!" Wo, therefore, unto him who has a
> large farm, particularly when others possess none.

The first session of the First Congress continued until September 29, 1789, and the second session began on January 4, 1790, and adjourned on August 12. In December 1790, the seat of government was removed from New York to Philadelphia, to remain there ten years, pending the erection of government buildings in the new city of Washington. In Philadelphia, the First Congress held its third session, continuing from December 6, 1790, until the following March 4. In its sessions, the First Congress accomplished a tremendous amount of important work, establishing a stable government for the nation and funding the national debt.

Members of the Second Congress were not chosen until three years after the election of the First Congress. General Muhlenberg was not elected to the Second Congress, though his brother, Frederick A., now living in Philadelphia, was returned. The latter, however, was not re-elected Speaker of the House. The election of congressmen by districts took place in Pennsylvania on October 11, 1791, and the Second Congress met shortly thereafter, on October 24. Citizens of Montgomery and Chester Counties, which then constituted a congressional district, held a meeting at Warren Tavern, Chester County, on October 4 to select a candidate for Congress. The matter was submitted to a committee composed of thirteen men from each county, and in the evening, they reported that their vote was: General Muhlenberg, 9; Thomas Ross, a Norristown lawyer, 8; William Moore, former provost of the College and Academy of Philadelphia, 4; Israel Jacobs, of Montgomery County, 3; John Hannum, 2. Though Muhlenberg was thus offered as the choice of the two counties, Israel Jacobs, who received only three votes in the Warren Tavern caucus, was elected.

Israel Jacobs, who was victorious over General Muhlenberg, was a Quaker living at what is now Mont Clare, Montgomery County, five miles south of Muhlenberg's home at Trappe and in the same township. Jacobs had been a member of the Pennsylvania Assembly, and at the time of the Revolution, he had aided the American cause so far as his Quaker principles would permit. He was the only Quaker member of the Second Congress, and he was conspicuous because of his broad-brimmed hat and Quaker garb.

One year after the choice of members of the Second Congress, those for the Third Congress were chosen, though they were not to go into office until more than a year later. Eleven members of the House were elected on a statewide ticket in Pennsylvania, and one of them was General Muhlenberg. A nominating meeting was held in Lancaster on September 20, 1792, when the following candidates were proposed: Thomas Fitzsimmons, Thomas Scott, Frederick A. Muhlenberg, William Irvine, James Armstrong, Thomas Hartley, Daniel Hiester, John W. Kittera, Henry Wynkoop, William Bingham, William Findley, Samuel Sitgreaves, and General Peter Muhlenberg. Of these, the following were elected on October 9, 1792: Fitzsimmons, Scott, F. A. Muhlenberg, General Peter Muhlenberg, Irvine, Armstrong, Hartley, Hiester, and

Findley. Andrew Gregg and John Smiley, who were on an opposition ticket, also were elected.

When the Third Congress began its sessions, in Congress Hall, Philadelphia, December 2, 1793, Frederick A. Muhlenberg was for the second time chosen the Speaker. Congress Hall, still standing at Chestnut and Sixth Streets, adjoining Independence Hall, was built in 1787-9 for the use of the county courts, but was turned over to Congress when Philadelphia became the capital for ten years. The House of Representatives convened on the first floor and the Senate on the second. In this session, General Muhlenberg was appointed a member of a special committee to prepare a bill for completing and supporting the military establishment.

Foreign complications due to the war between France and England and the aggressions of both these nations against the commerce of the United States claimed the serious attention of the President and Congress. Among the followers of Jefferson were many who wanted to align the United States with France against England, in return for the aid of France to the United States in the American Revolution. But Washington insisted upon a policy of strict neutrality.

The first session of the Third Congress continued until June 9, 1794, and the second from November 3, 1794, until March 3, 1795. In 1794 there was a reapportionment of congressional districts in Pennsylvania dividing the state into twelve districts. Montgomery, Bucks, and Northampton Counties constituted a district, which was entitled to two members. The Federalist Party candidates were General Samuel Sitgreaves, of Northampton, and James Morris, of Montgomery County. In addition, Robert Loller, of Hatboro, Montgomery County, was an independent Federalist candidate. The Republican Party, comprising the followers of Jefferson, had as its candidates General Muhlenberg and John Richards, both of Montgomery County. Ordinarily, the Federalists would have been in control of the district. Robert Loller's independent candidacy, however, complicated the results and led to a contest in the House of Representatives.

The Whiskey Rebellion was in progress in western Pennsylvania at the time of the election, in October 1794, and the Pennsylvania militia was in the field to subdue the uprising. According to a law enacted to meet this situation, the votes of the militiamen were to be taken in their camp and sent to the counties whence they came. Return judges of the three counties constituting the congressional district were to meet on November 15 to compute the vote for House of Representatives. When they met, the vote of the militiamen for Montgomery and Berks Counties had not yet arrived. Consequently, Governor Mifflin refused to certify the election based on the returns sent to him.

It was clear that General Sitgreaves had been elected. But the vote for Morris and Richards was very close. Muhlenberg was defeated, his vote running considerably behind that of his associate, Richards. The clerk of the House of Representatives recognized Morris as the winner, along with Sitgreaves. Thereupon Richards instituted a contest in the House, and the matter was referred to a committee. The committee first reported in favor of Morris, but the report was recommitted, and in January 1796, a second report was presented declaring that, after rejecting certain defective votes, Morris had received 1779 votes in the district and Richards 1791. Richards was therefore elected. This report was adopted, and Richards was seated.

The small number of votes cast in those three large counties was indicative not only of the sparseness of the population but also of the indisposition of many citizens to exercise their right to vote. In Montgomery County, there were but three polling places, and many farmers did not care to undertake a long journey to vote.

While still a member of the Third Congress, General Muhlenberg was nominated as the Republican Party's candidate for United States Senator from Pennsylvania, to succeed Robert Morris. The election took place in the state Legislature on February 26, 1795. But as the Federalists were largely in the majority, they had no difficulty in selecting their candidate, William Bingham, of Philadelphia. He received 58 votes, to 35 for Muhlenberg.

General Muhlenberg was chosen as a presidential elector from Pennsylvania in 1796 when Thomas Jefferson was the candidate of the Republicans and John Adams that of the Federalists. The vote in Pennsylvania was so close that among the electors named both parties were represented. General Muhlenberg, Republican, and Colonel Samuel Miles, Federalist, both from Montgomery County, were chosen. Muhlenberg, of course, voted for Jefferson, but Adams was elected.

General Muhlenberg was again proposed for the United States Senate in the Pennsylvania Legislature in February 1797, but James Ross, of Allegheny County, the sitting member, was re-elected.

## War with France Threatened

In October 1797, General Muhlenberg was elected one of the four members of the Pennsylvania House of Representatives from Montgomery County for a one-year term. This election was the first important victory of the Republican Party in Montgomery County, three of the four representatives chosen were of that party. General Muhlenberg was in attendance at the Legislature's sessions for 122 days, for which he received $3 a day, and $5.20 mileage was allowed him for traveling expenses from his home in Trappe to the state capital, in Philadelphia.

This was the period when the United States nearly became involved in a war with France. The French Revolution had been followed by a war between France and England. France looked for American support in return for the aid which America had received from France in the American Revolution. But although there was much enthusiasm in the United States for the revolutionary movement in France, the government felt it to be the policy of wisdom to remain neutral, for it was in no way prepared to undertake another war. Jay's treaty with England, whereby some of the long-standing differences between that country and the United States were adjusted, was offensive to France. Both England and France adopted an arbitrary attitude toward America, seizing American ships that were accused of carrying contraband goods. Three successive French ministers to the United States persistently meddled with politics here to obtain support for France. Finally came the humiliating treatment accorded the three American envoys sent to France in 1797 to endeavor to harmonize relations, when it became clear that nothing could be done without bribery, and then the American watchword was sounded. "Millions for defense but not one cent for tribute."

Before the crisis was reached, William Maclay introduced a resolution in the Pennsylvania Legislature, in March 1798, opposing war with any European nation. General Muhlenberg voted with the Republicans for the resolution, which was adopted, 37 to 33. Commenting on the situation in the Legislature, Muhlenberg wrote thus to Israel Bringhurst, of Trappe, in a letter dated March 26, 1798:

> Fate and destiny, combined with the aristocrats, are hurrying us
> precipitately into a ruinous and bloody war, and the chance of
> escape is a slender one indeed. You will see by the papers that
> an attempt was made in our House to instruct our Senators in
> Congress to maintain peace if possible, but, strange to say, all the
> Quakers, Old Tories, etc., voted against it so that they are for war
> and the fighting men for peace.

News of the futile attempt of the American envoys to treat with France arrived later in 1798 and greatly intensified the war feeling. Congress authorized the enlistment of an army, with George Washington commander-in-chief, and the navy was enlarged. Several conflicts occurred between America and French warships.

Once more, General Muhlenberg was elected to Congress—in October 1798. The district still comprised Montgomery, Bucks, and Northampton Counties. This Sixth Congress was the last to meet in Philadelphia and the first to convene in Washington. Its sessions began on December 2, 1799, in Congress Hall, Philadelphia.

On December 18, news of the death of Washington at Mount Vernon four days earlier reached Congress in Philadelphia. The following day Congress appointed a committee to arrange for memorial services, and General Muhlenberg was a member of the committee, the chairman being John Marshall, of Virginia, later Chief Justice of the United States

Supreme Court. No doubt it was through General Muhlenberg that arrangements were made to hold the official ceremonies on December 27 in Zion Lutheran Church, which had the largest auditorium in the city and which church he as a young minister had helped to dedicate in 1769. The committee, in its report, besides outlining the plans for the memorial service on the 27th, also recommended that a monument to Washington be erected in the city of Washington and that Washington's family be asked to permit his burial at the monument.

During the day of mourning, sixteen cannon were fired to announce the day. This was followed by one cannon every half hour until 11:30 am, when the ceremonial funeral procession escorted an empty bier from Sixth and Chestnut Streets to Zion Lutheran Church, where Bishop William White of Christ Church conducted the service. General Henry "Lighthorse Harry" Lee, the most prominent close relative of Washington's, through the first lady Martha Washington's Custis line, gave the eulogy. While hastily written and poorly delivered, it contained the immortal line: "First in War, First in Peace, First in the Hearts of his Countrymen." Eight years later, Lee fathered Robert E. Lee.

Though the Republican Party had been making great gains throughout the country, the Federalists still had a small majority in this Congress. The war danger having passed, Congress, in February 1800, voted to discontinue enlistments, and the following month it ordered the discharge of the extra troops enrolled in the army.

General Muhlenberg was appointed a major general of the Pennsylvania militia, on April 22, 1800, commanding the Militia of Montgomery and Bucks Counties. In the case of war, the militia would have been added to the army. However, by the end of the century, the likelihood of war faded, and on July 11, 1801, General Muhlenberg resigned his office of major general.

The federal capital was transferred from Philadelphia to the new city of Washington in July 1800, and on November 17, following the second session of the Sixth Congress began in the new federal buildings. It became the duty of the House, early in 1801, to choose the next President, for in the electoral college Thomas Jefferson and Aaron Burr both had the same number of votes. They were nominees of the Republican Party. Electors then voted for two candidates without specifying whether either was preferred for President or Vice President. The tie made it necessary for the House to determine the issue, voting by states, and Thomas Jefferson was chosen, though thirty-six ballots were necessary. General Muhlenberg voted for Jefferson on every ballot.

There is a story, apparently coming from General Muhlenberg himself, that in this crisis, the Jefferson followers suspected the opposition of plotting to vest the presidency in the chief justice of the Supreme Court, that they determined to arm their men and prevent such a step by force if necessary and that General Muhlenberg was selected to command the Jeffersonians in their march upon the capital. Jefferson, Madison, Monroe, and Thomas McKean, it was said, were involved in the project. Whatever was contemplated, the election of Jefferson in the House averted further entanglements. The Sixth Congress closed its sessions on March 3, 1801.

## The Perkiomen Bridge Lottery

In the closing years of the century, General Muhlenberg was engaged in an undertaking for an important public improvement near his home at Trappe, which remains to recall his name. He supervised a lottery to raise funds for constructing a bridge over Perkiomen Creek, where the highway from Philadelphia to Reading crossed, two miles below Trappe. The bridge is a noble example of eighteenth-century masonry, attracting attention by the beauty of its lines and its picturesque setting.

As early as 1794, the State Legislature of Pennsylvania appropriated £2000 for building a bridge at this place, and the next year Montgomery County gave a like sum. It was not worthwhile beginning work with that amount. In 1796, the grand jury of the county sanctioned another appropriation of £2000, but the court disallowed it. In response to a new appeal to the Legislature, a common method of that time was adopted to meet the situation. The Legislature authorized the holding of a lottery to raise $20,000 for the bridge.

The act that was passed provided for the appointment of a commission to conduct the lottery. The commissioners were to devise a plan and submit it to the governor for approval. They were to settle every three months with the county treasurer, reporting the number of tickets sold and paying over the proceeds. The commissioners were required to give bonds, and the county treasurer was placed under similar obligations regarding the lottery money. It was the duty of the lottery commissioners furthermore to conduct the drawing, certify the list of prizes to the county treasurer, and publish the winning numbers in newspapers in Philadelphia, Reading, and Harrisburg. Winners were to present their tickets to the county treasurer and receive their prizes.

The commissioners named were General Peter Muhlenberg; John Richards, who had once defeated Muhlenberg for Congress; Francis Swaine, General Muhlenberg's brother-in-law; Samuel Bair; Moses Hobson; Frederick Conrad; Samuel Markley; Robert Kennedy; and John Elliot.

The commissioners held several meetings in a Norristown tavern, General Muhlenberg being chairman. In that capacity, his name appeared on the lottery tickets, of which 20,000 were issued in two series. For the first series, the drawing began on July 17, 1797, and continued twenty-one days. The first prize was $3000, the second prize $1000, and the third prize $500. The last ten numbers drawn received $250 each. Drawings for the second series began November 1, 1798, and continued for twenty-five days. This time the prizes were $1000, $500, and ten at $150 each.

The proceeds from the lottery being insufficient to pay for building the bridge, the Legislature, in 1799, permitted the collection of tolls at the bridge until the entire cost should be defrayed. The bridge was opened in 1799, and a toll was collected for five years.

## His Home at Trappe

In the last decade of the eighteenth century, General Muhlenberg was several times proposed as a candidate for Governor of Pennsylvania. But he was disinclined to oppose Thomas Mifflin, who was twice re-elected in that period, nor did he wish to undertake the candidacy in 1799, when Thomas McKean was chosen. In a letter which he wrote from Trappe on February 4, 1799, to Colonel Taverner Beale, of Virginia, with whom he had been associated in Revolutionary days, General Muhlenberg mentioned that the Democratic-Republicans, or Jefferson men, were soliciting him to run for governor, and the leaders among the German voters were likewise importuning him. "But," he added, "I cannot get my own consent."

The letter revealed that he had not abandoned his youthful love for hunting and fishing, which had elicited the disapprobation of his father. Colonel Beale had invited Muhlenberg to visit Virginia to indulge in these sports. General Muhlenberg, in his reply, admitted that the invitation was alluring to him, but he hesitated about accepting it. The pike in the Ohio River, on the borders of which stream he owned a great tract of land, he wrote, "are much larger than those with you, and tho' the pike in Jacksons River are larger than those in the Perkiomen; still they are not so sweet."

Evidently, General Muhlenberg would sometimes go fishing in the nearby Perkiomen Creek, which is still a favorite resort of the angler, though the oldest inhabitant of the present time does not recall that a pike was ever seen in the waters of that stream.

Regarding his family and personal affairs, General Muhlenberg, in his letter to Colonel Beale, continued: "I still live at the Trappe, in the house my father lived when you were here. Mr. Swaine lives in the first house below me. He keeps a store and is a magistrate. My family consists of my wife and myself, Harry, Hetty, Peter, Mary Ann, and Frank." Harry was then a senior lieutenant in the corps of artillery of the regular army and was stationed at West Point. Hetty was with her maternal grandmother in Philadelphia, and the other children were with their parents at Trappe.

As to himself, General Muhlenberg wrote: "I am heartily tired of politics." Mentioning the 10,000 acres of excellent land he owned on the Scioto River, in what is now the state of Ohio, he added: "There I wish to spend the remainder of my days." But his mother, who was still living, objected to his going to what was regarded as the Far West, and his wife's mother also protested the suggestion because Mrs. Muhlenberg was her only daughter. Yet neither really required his assistance, he said. His mother-in-law, he wrote, "has the whole estate in hand and adds to it considerably every year."

General Muhlenberg's popularity among his neighbors is attested by the fact that he presided at a Fourth of July celebration held in 1799 on the banks of the Perkiomen. Like most such celebrations in those times, this was a political demonstration in which the militia participated. According to a newspaper report, it was attended by "a large and respectable number of citizens." After a military drill in the morning, dinner was served, and, adhering to the customs of the times, many toasts were drunk. A meeting followed at one of the taverns in Trappe at which Thomas McKean's candidacy for governor was indorsed.

## Chosen United States Senator

Though "heartily tired" of politics, General Muhlenberg's political career was not yet ended. At the election in October 1800, he was returned to the United States House of Representatives as one of the two members from a district consisting of Montgomery, Bucks, Northampton, and Wayne Counties. The term for which he was thus chosen was to begin in December 1801. But he did not take his seat in the House because on February 18, 1801, the Legislature of Pennsylvania, in session in Lancaster, then the state capital, elected General Muhlenberg to represent the state in the United States Senate.

The Republicans dominated the Legislature, but a split occurred in that party. Dr. George Logan received most of the Republican votes for United States Senator, while a minority joined with the Federalists in electing General Muhlenberg. He received forty-six votes, fifteen of which were cast by Republicans. This was a majority of one vote over Dr. Logan. The latter, who was a grandson of the noted James Logan, provincial secretary of Pennsylvania, and who lived at Stenton, the Logan homestead near Germantown, had been much in the public eye since 1798, when he visited France and endeavored to avert war between the United States and France. The Federalists resented this as unwarranted interference by a private citizen in national affairs, and in consequence, Congress passed what was known as the Logan Act, which is still in effect and which forbids meddling with international affairs by a private citizen.

General Muhlenberg sat in the United States Senate for just two days. The Sixth Congress came to an end on March 3, 1801, and General Muhlenberg was regularly in attendance in the House. The inauguration of President Thomas Jefferson took place on March 4, and the same day the Senate of the Seventh Congress convened in special session. One of the new members to whom the oath of office was administered was General Muhlenberg. The ensuing day concluded the special session, which had been called only to confirm appointments by the new President.

## Appointed to Federal Offices

In June 1801, President Jefferson, in recognition of General Muhlenberg's unwavering support of Jefferson's political aspirations and principles, appointed him supervisor of internal revenue for Pennsylvania. Thereupon General Muhlenberg resigned as a senator. Governor Thomas McKean named Dr. Logan to fill the vacancy in the Senate, and the following December, the Legislature elected him for a full term.

While the dignities and honors of a member of the United States Senate were immeasurably beyond those of any revenue official, it is evident that Muhlenberg was not seeking dignity and honors but preferred an office nearer his home and yielding a comfortable salary. Life in the new capital city of Washington, with its highways deep in mud or dust and its few lodging houses primitive and destitute of comforts, was beset with many inconveniences.

After about a year in the revenue service, President Jefferson, in July 1802, made General Muhlenberg collector of the port in Philadelphia, which was one of the most remunerative offices in the President's gift. Philadelphia was then the leading port on the Atlantic coast, and the duties of the customs official called for probity and trustworthiness of the highest type. This office Muhlenberg held until his death.

As the collector of the port, general Muhlenberg's duties required his presence in Philadelphia. In those times, it was a day's journey from Trappe to Philadelphia. He, therefore, made his home in Philadelphia, selling his house and twenty-one acres of land at Trappe, in 1802, to his brother-in-law, the Reverend Dr. John Christopher Kunze, of New York. The house still stands, being on the northeast side of Trappe's Main Street, opposite Saint Luke's Reformed Church, and a short distance below an intersecting road to Rahns. Early in the twentieth century, it was the home of John S. McHarg and family.

General Muhlenberg's mother died on August 23, 1802, in Norristown, at the home of her daughter, Mary Catherine, wife of General Francis Swaine. General Swaine was at that time clerk of the courts and prothonotary of Montgomery County. Mrs. Muhlenberg was buried alongside her husband, close to the walls of Augustus Church, in Trappe.

General Muhlenberg continued to be a powerful factor in Pennsylvania politics. The old-time Federalists had almost disappeared in Pennsylvania, but the followers of Jefferson, known as Republicans or Democratic-Republicans, were often split into factions, and about such splits, most of the political campaigns of that time revolved. Early in the new century, a movement arose for a revision of the state constitution, and this was for a time a political issue, resulting in the organization of a new political party which existed for a few years. Muhlenberg supported Governor McKean in opposing constitutional revision. Those taking this attitude and favoring the re-election of McKean as governor formed what was known as the Constitutional Republican Party, the members being dubbed Tertium Quids. General Muhlenberg was elected president of the party organization and Matthew Carey secretary, though the dominant personage in the movement was Alexander J. Dallas, Pennsylvania's Secretary of the Commonwealth. McKean was re-elected governor in 1805 by about a 5000-vote majority over the Republican candidate, Simon Snyder. Having accomplished its mission, the Constitutional Republican Party soon ceased to exist.

While he was much engaged in political activities at a time of intense partisanship, when each side attributed every form of evil and depravity to its opponents, yet General Muhlenberg had so firmly won the esteem of the public that he escaped the denunciation which was usually let loose in floods in every political campaign of that period.

## President of the German Society

In Philadelphia, General Muhlenberg was again in close association with many friends of earlier times among the large German population. Two groups in which he was active were the German Society and the German Lutheran Church.

The German Society of Pennsylvania had been organized in 1764 to afford relief to German immigrants in distress. It has maintained an existence ever since, though, in late years, it has functioned chiefly as a social, literary, and historical society. General Muhlenberg became a member in 1783, upon returning to Pennsylvania after the Revolution. In 1787, he was elected a member of the board of directors and vice president, and the following year he became president, serving one year. His brother, Frederick A. Muhlenberg, was president from 1790 until 1797. In 1802, General Muhlenberg was again made president, and he held the office up to his death.

In 1806, the society built a hall for its use on the west side of Seventh Street, between Market and Chestnut. Up to that time, it had been meeting in the German Lutheran schoolhouse on Cherry Street. The site for the hall had been bought before the Revolution, but the war necessitated postponement of building plans. As president, General Muhlenberg had a conspicuous part in the dedication of the new building on April 9, 1807.

## Fosters English Lutheran Services

In the old German Lutheran congregation of Saint Michael's and Zion, of which his father had been a pastor and whose members had been so favorably impressed with his first sermons, General Muhlenberg gave his support to the minority that was trying in vain to make provision for services in the English language.

For many years this Lutheran congregation had been the largest religious group in Philadelphia. But now the young people no longer continued to use the German language, and the church was losing them. In February 1801, certain members petitioned the church authorities to engage an English as well as a German minister. No action was taken. In December 1802, permission was granted to the Reverend Henry E. Muhlenberg, a brother of General Muhlenberg, to preach an English sermon in Zion Church. Further concessions were refused, and on February 14, following the congregation at a meeting, he decided not to introduce the English language in its services.

On March 14, 1804, those desiring English services held a largely attended meeting at which General Muhlenberg presided. As a result, an address signed by General Muhlenberg was printed and sent to all members of the congregation. This set forth that many members of the church did not understand German and urged that some services be held in English. "The evangelical doctrine," the address declared, "does not depend upon this or that language." Luther, it was pointed out, wanted the gospel preached in the language of the people. To hold the young people to the Lutheran faith, it was essential that English services be held.

Still, most of the congregation refused to yield. The minority then appealed to the Lutheran Ministerium of Pennsylvania, at its annual meeting for 1805, which was held in Germantown in June. A letter was presented asking either that English services be held at times in Saint

Michael's or Zion Churches or else that a new congregation, entirely English, be constituted. The letter was signed by Lorenz Seckel, George A. Becker, Johannes Graff, and Peter Muhlenberg. After deliberating upon the question, the Ministerium ruled that it must remain a German body, but that Lutherans who did not understand German might form English congregations, which the Ministerium would recognize.

The next step in the Philadelphia congregation was taken at the annual meeting on January 6, 1806, when those appealing for English services tried to elect church officials favorable to their side. In this, they failed. Two days later, they met at the home of John Hay. The outcome of this and several other meetings was a decision to establish a society for encouraging English Lutheran services and to obtain the use of the Academy building for English catechetical classes. Adopting the name of The Evangelical Lutheran Association in and near the City of Philadelphia, the members declared they did not seek to occasion a split in the old congregation, but they were determined to call a minister who would preach both in English and German and catechize children in English. He was not to supplant the German minister but to work with him in the parish. At a meeting on May 27, a constitution was adopted, which fifty persons signed, one of them being Peter Muhlenberg.

The plan proposed was not practicable. The movement resulted quickly in the establishment of a new English-speaking congregation. Saint John's Church was the first English Lutheran congregation to attain permanency in America. The Reverend Philip F. Mayer, a native of New York City, was called to pastor in June 1806. He had been trained for the ministry under the Reverend Dr. Kunze, General Muhlenberg's brother-in-law, and when called to Philadelphia, he had a charge in Athens, New York. The need for an English minister was proved when Pastor Mayer on Maundy Thursday, 1807, confirmed 138 persons. A church was built on the north side of Race Street, between Fifth and Sixth, and was consecrated on June 19, 1809. General Muhlenberg did not live to witness the dedication.

Even after the withdrawal of the English-speaking members from the German congregation, in 1806, German dominance was not altogether assured in the parent congregation, and during ensuing years, frequent controversies occurred over the language question. The majority insisted the gospel could be adequately preached only in German, and there were times when, apparently, they dreamed of making Philadelphia a German city. In 1816, certain members were tried in court on the charge of conspiring to prevent the introduction of English in the German congregation. They were convicted, but Governor Snyder pardoned them. Eventually, Saint Michael's Church was abandoned, but Zion Church survived with a wholly German congregation.

General Muhlenberg also maintained an interest in Augustus Church, Trappe, though he lived in Philadelphia. Under his direction, the congregation was incorporated in 1805. He paid the costs involved. On September 10, 1807, less than a month before his death, he wrote the congregation as follows:

> By John Markley, Esq., I transmit the sum of $50 presented to you by my son, Henry M. Muhlenberg, and myself. I have likewise in my last will and testament bequeathed unto you a bank share in the Bank of Philadelphia annually, which my executors are directed to purchase and pay to the congregation within twelve months after my decease. This donation of money and this bequest are intended as a small capital, the interest arising from which shall be wholly and solely appropriated to keep in decent order and repair the burying ground now belonging to the congregation. When this annual repair is completed, and a surplus should then remain, the corporation shall then be at liberty to expend the said surplus in any repairs to the church they may think proper.

In accordance with the terms of the will, as indicated in the letter, General Muhlenberg's executors on December 12, 1809, paid Augustus congregation $125, accruing from the sale of the bank stock mentioned.

## His Last Days

The only edition of the *Philadelphia Directory* in which General Muhlenberg's name appears was that for 1807, when he was listed at 124 North Fourth Street. This, no doubt, was his office as collector of customs.

On June 17, 1806, he bought from Samuel Emery a house, together with twenty-one acres and fifty-nine perches of land, bordering the Schuylkill River, below Grays Ferry Road, in what was then Passyunk Township, in the southern part of Philadelphia County. It was a pleasing rural district in those times. A subsequent description shows that there were on the place a "handsome two-story brick house, a good frame barn, a coach house, a frame two-story tenement house, and a fish house," and attached to the farm was a fishery in the Schuylkill, declared to be one of the best in the river. The land was described as "in the highest state of cultivation."

But General Muhlenberg was destined to enjoy the charms of this rural retreat for only a little more than a year. The same year that he bought the place, on October 23, his wife died. She was in her fifty-sixth year. His own death occurred on his sixty-first birthday anniversary, October 1, 1807, at 8 A.M. Death was due to a liver affection from which he had suffered much distress at intervals ever since the Georgia campaign of 1776.

The funeral took place at 6 o'clock the morning after his death. As the cortège passed the hall of the German Society, on Seventh Street, which General Muhlenberg had helped to dedicate a few months before, the members of the society joined the mourners and accompanied the funeral to Zion Church, at Fourth and Cherry Streets, where services were held. The funeral then continued to Augustus Church, Trappe, where the burial took place with military honors, "amidst a large concourse of respectable citizens," as a newspaper of the time recorded. The grave is with those of his father and other members of the family close to the walls of the historic old church, immediately back of the pulpit. A large marble slab covering the grave is thus inscribed:

Sacred to the memory of General Peter Muhlenberg, born October 1, 1746, died October 1, 1807. He was brave in the field, faithful in the cabinet, honorable in all his transactions, a sincere friend, and an honest man.

By his will, which he signed on July 18, 1807, General Muhlenberg directed that his lands in Ohio and Kentucky be sold and the proceeds divided among his four living children. The executors, general Francis Swaine and John Graff, were directed to emancipate Kitty, a negro slave, while Hannah, an indentured servant, was to be exonerated from the remainder of her time. The census of 1790 showed that General Muhlenberg then owned one negro slave. There were then 3737 slaves in Pennsylvania.

One of General Muhlenberg's sons, his namesake, Peter, who was born in 1787, adopted a military career, serving in the United States Army from 1808 until 1821 and advancing through the ranks from first lieutenant to major. He was engaged in the War of 1812 and in various Indian wars. His death occurred in 1844.

Another son, Francis Swaine, born in 1795, practiced law in Reading, Pennsylvania, was private secretary to Governor Joseph Hiester, of Pennsylvania, 1820-3, then lived in Pickaway County, Ohio, where he was elected to the House of Representatives of Ohio and later to the United States House of Representatives. He died at the age of 36.

General Muhlenberg's daughter, Hester married Dr. Isaac Hiester, of Reading, Pennsylvania, in 1810, and lived until 1872. A son of this couple, William Muhlenberg Hiester, was speaker of the Pennsylvania Senate, 1852-5, and Secretary of the Commonwealth of Pennsylvania, 1858-61.

A son, Charles Frederick, born in 1778, was drowned in the Delaware River at Philadelphia May 31, 1795, when a boat he was rowing collided with another boat and was upset.

Other children of General Muhlenberg were: Henry Meyer, born 1775, died 1806, no issue, and Mary Ann, born 1793, died 1805.

## Statue in the National Capitol

When Congress created Statuary Hall, in the national capitol, and each state was asked to place therein the figures of its two most outstanding citizens, Pennsylvania chose General Peter Muhlenberg and Robert Fulton, the one representing the great tide of German settlers and the other coming from the Scotch-Irish element that also was so conspicuous in pioneering days. Muhlenberg stood for Pennsylvania's military and political leadership, and Fulton, who made the steamship practicable, typified applied science and invention.

By an act of the Pennsylvania Legislature in 1877, Governor Hartranft was authorized to appoint a commission to erect Pennsylvania's statues in the capitol in Washington. Former Senator Simon Cameron was made the chairman of the commission. Miss Blanche Nevin, of Lancaster, was engaged to create the Muhlenberg statue in Carrara marble. She received $7500 for her work. Because of a delay on the part of the Legislature in making the necessary appropriations, about ten years elapsed before the statues were placed in position.

The Muhlenberg statue was Miss Nevin's most important achievement in sculpture. She was a daughter of the Reverend John W. Nevin, a Reformed clergyman who was a leader in the exposition of what was known as the "Mercersburg theology" in the controversies which rent his denomination in the middle of the nineteenth century. In the statue, General Muhlenberg is presented arrayed in military uniform.

On the grounds behind the Philadelphia Art Museum, in the Anne d'Harnoncourt Sculpture Garden, there is a heroic statue of General Muhlenberg in military garb. The statue, the work of J. Otto Schweizer, a Philadelphia sculptor, was originally placed on City Hall Plaza on German Day, October 6, 1910, and was a gift of the German societies of Philadelphia. Incidental to the dedication, there was a parade of the German organizations of Philadelphia and the Ancient Order of Hibernians, together with United States Marines, details from the National Guard of Pennsylvania, and members of the Grand Army of the Republic.

General Louis Wagner presided, and addresses were made by Dr. C. J. Hexamer, Judge William H. Staake, Mayer John Edgar Reyburn, and Dr. Arthur Mudra, German consul. On the front of the pedestal is a bas relief in bronze portraying the scene at the Woodstock church when Peter Muhlenberg bade farewell to the pulpit to enter the army. Due to the construction of the subway under and about City Hall, the statue was removed in 1928 to Reyburn Plaza at the entrance to the Parkway, north of City Hall, where it remained until it went into storage in 1961 for several decades.

Henry Muhlenberg house in Trappe, Pennsylvania, later owned by Peter Muhlenberg

The Henry Muhlenberg house how it looks today

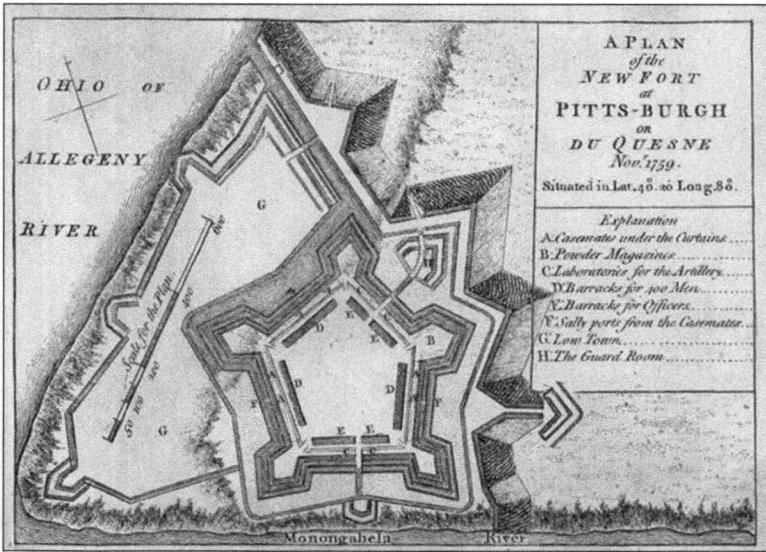

Fort Pitt

General and Governor Thomas Mifflin

Daniel Hiester

Reverend Dr. John Christopher Kunze

Margaret Henrietta
Muhlenberg

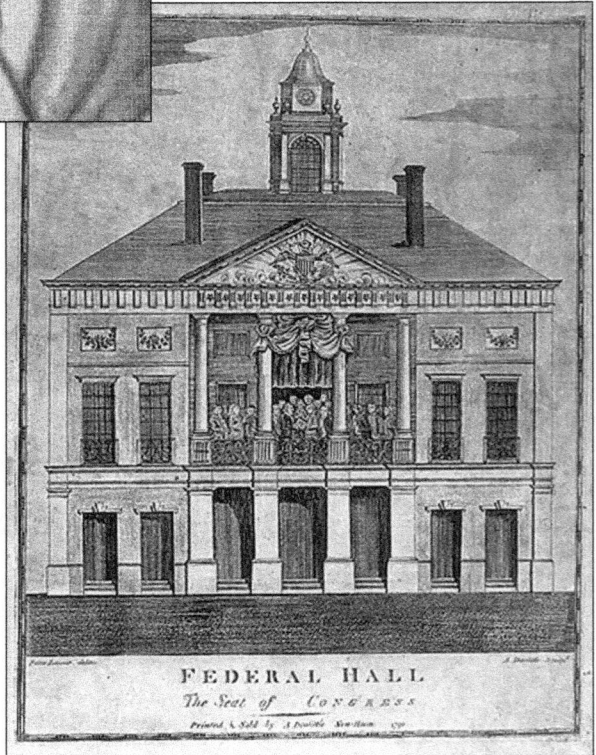

Federal Hall, New York, New York

Frederick A. Muhlenberg, brother of Peter Muhlenberg

Charles Thomson

Washington's Inauguration in New York City

Joseph Hiester

Warren Tavern, Chester County, Pennsylvania

Israel Jacobs

Congress Hall, Philadelphia, Pennsylvania

William Maclay

Washington's memorial service at Zion Lutheran Church in
Philadelphia, Pennsylvania

George Washington death scene at Mount Vernon, Virginia

Washington's honorary funeral procession in Philadelphia, Pennsylvania

John Marshall

Aaron Burr

Perkiomen Bridge

Gotthilf Henry Ernst Muhlenberg

Hester "Hetty" Muhlenberg Hiester

Dr. George Logan

Alexander J. Dallas

Simon Snyder

German Society of Pennsylvania

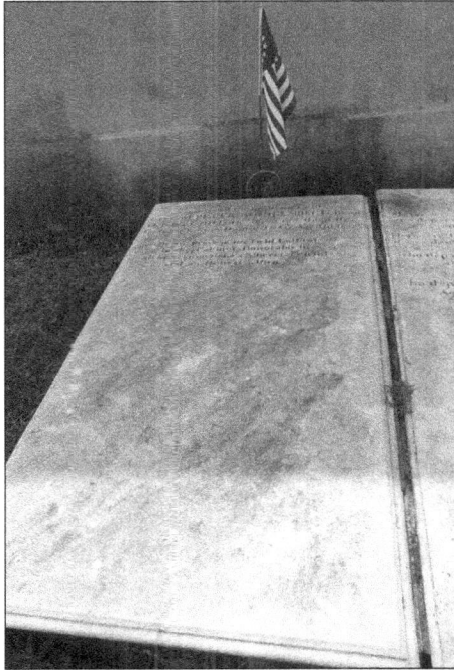

The grave of Peter Muhlenberg at Augustus
Church, Trappe, Pennsylvania

Francis Swaine Muhlenberg

William Muhlenberg Hiester

Statue of Peter Muhlenberg in
Statuary Hall in the national Capitol
in Washington, D.C.

Statue of Peter Muhlenberg
along Connecticut Avenue in
Washington, D.C.

Statue of Peter Muhlenberg in
Woodstock, Virginia

Peter Muhlenberg Statue when it stood in front of Philadelphia's City Hall

Detail of the Peter Muhlenberg statue

# V

# DISTINGUISHED MEMBERS
## OF THE
## MUHLENBERG FAMILY

### Frederick A. Muhlenberg

In telling the story of Peter Muhlenberg, numerous allusions have been made to his brother, Frederick A. Muhlenberg. Both brothers forsook the ministry at the time of the Revolution, Peter entering the army, and Frederick becoming a leader in civic life. After the Revolution, both were powerful for many years in the politics of Pennsylvania. John Adams blamed them for bringing about the virtual extinction of the Federalist Party in Pennsylvania in the last decade of the eighteenth century.

Returning from Europe where they had been educated for the ministry at Halle, in Germany, Frederick and his brother Henry were ordained to the Lutheran ministry on October 25, 1770. Frederick was then not yet 21 years old, and Henry was still younger. Frederick's first service in the ministry was as assistant to his brother-in-law, the Reverend Christopher E. Schulze, in the Tulpehocken region of Berks County, Pennsylvania. Later, for a short time, he was stationed in Lebanon, Pennsylvania. Then in 1773, he assumed the pastorate of a church in New York City that had been founded some years before. When the Revolution opened, Frederick A. Muhlenberg sided with the Americans, which made it expedient for him to leave New York when the British took possession. In

1776, he assisted his father, and the following year he took charge of the New Hanover congregation, several miles west of Trappe, which was the oldest Lutheran congregation of German origin in America.

Early in 1779, he decided to abandon the ministry, and in March of that year, the State Assembly in filling three Pennsylvania vacancies in the Continental Congress, elected Frederick A. Muhlenberg to one of them. He was chosen for a full term in Congress at the ensuing election. In Congress he was chairman of the medical committee, directing the hospital service in the army. In October 1780, he was elected to the Pennsylvania Assembly, and when that body organized, he was made speaker, which office he filled during three sessions of the Assembly. In 1783, he was elected a member of a peculiar Pennsylvania institution, the board of censors, and became chairman of the board. From 1784 until 1789 he was a justice of the peace at Trappe, and in that capacity, was one of the board of judges of the new county of Montgomery, formed in 1784, being president judge for the first year. He was also the first register of wills and recorder of deeds of the new county. Being elected a member of the Pennsylvania convention to ratify the new federal constitution of 1787, he was made president of the convention.

He was elected to the First, Second, Third, and Fourth Congresses under the Constitution and was speaker of the First and Third. About 1790, he made his home in Philadelphia on North Second Street. He was a member of a mercantile firm in Philadelphia and later part-owner of a sugar refinery.

After his congressional career closed, Governor McKean, of Pennsylvania, appointed him collector of the General Land Office of the state, in 1800, whereupon he removed to Lancaster, then the capital of Pennsylvania. There he died on June 4, 1801, when 51 years old. He had grown extremely corpulent, and death resulted from a stroke of apoplexy. Burial took place in the grounds of Trinity Lutheran Church, Lancaster, though he was later moved to Woodlawn Cemetery in that city.

William A. Muhlenberg (1796-1877), a grandson of Frederick A. Muhlenberg, became a distinguished clergyman of the Episcopal church.

He grew to maturity in Philadelphia in the period when the Lutheran church refused to make provisions for English services, and hence his parents permitted him to attend the Episcopal church, in which he was confirmed. He entered the ministry of that church in 1817 and was rector of a church in Lancaster, Pennsylvania. In 1846, he went to New York City, where he founded the Episcopal Church of the Holy Communion and the first Episcopal sisterhood in America, Saint Luke's Hospital, and Saint Johnsland, the latter a Christian rural settlement with homes for boys and aged men. He wrote numerous favorite hymns, including "Savior Who Thy Flock Art Feeding" and "I Would Not Live Always." Largely through his efforts, the old building of Augustus Church, Trappe, was saved in 1860 after the congregation had decided it should be demolished.

## The Reverend Henry E. Muhlenberg

Of the three Muhlenberg brothers who entered the ministry, only Gottfried Henry Ernst remained a clergyman throughout his life. In maturity, he dropped his first name. After ordination, in his 20th year, he assisted his father, and in 1774, he became one of the pastors of the Philadelphia Lutheran congregation. From 1789 until his death in 1815, he was pastor of Trinity Church, Lancaster, Pennsylvania. Like his brothers, he gained distinction outside the pulpit, for he was one of the celebrated botanists of his time and wrote extensively on that subject.

A son of the Reverend Henry E. Muhlenberg, Henry Augustus Philip Muhlenberg (1782-1844), became a Lutheran minister and was the pastor of Trinity Church, Reading, Pennsylvania, from 1802 until 1827, resigning because of impaired health. In 1829 he was elected to the National House of Representatives, and by subsequent re-elections, he served until 1838 when he resigned. President Van Buren offered to appoint him Secretary of the Navy and then Minister to Russia, but he declined both offers, though he did accept a third tender, that of Minister to Austria. This post he held from 1838 until 1840. Three times he received the Democratic nomination for Governor of Pennsylvania. Twice he was defeated, and shortly after his third nomination he died.

Henry Augustus Muhlenberg (1823-1854), a son of Henry A. P. Muhlenberg, was a lawyer in Reading, Pennsylvania, a member of the Pennsylvania Senate, and was elected to the National House of Representatives in 1853, but died in Washington the following January.

## Other Branches of the Family

Eve Elizabeth Muhlenberg (1748-1808), eldest sister of the Muhlenberg brothers, in 1766 married the Reverend Christopher Emanuel Schulze, who was a Lutheran pastor in the Tulpehocken region of Berks County, Pennsylvania, from 1769 until his death. Their sons John Andrew Shulze (1775-1852), was a Lutheran pastor from 1796 until 1804, and then, like his distinguished uncles, he entered political life. He was a member of the State Legislature for four terms, a state senator and then governor of Pennsylvania for two terms, 1823 until 1829.

Margaret Henrietta Muhlenberg (1751-1831), another sister, married the Reverend John Christopher Kunze, Lutheran pastor in Philadelphia and New York, and a member of the faculty of Columbia College, New York. Mrs. Kunze was the last survivor of her generation.

Following is the record of the other brothers and sisters of General Muhlenberg:

- Mary Catherine (1755-1812) was the first wife of Francis Swaine, who was prominent in political affairs in Montgomery County, Pennsylvania, in the early nineteenth century, was the first president of the Bank of Montgomery County, Norristown, and was also a militia general.

- John Enoch Samuel, born 1758; John Charles, born 1760; Catherine Salome, born 1764; and Emanuel Samuel, born 1769, all died in infancy.

▦ Maria Salome (1766-1830) married Matthias Richards, who was a member of the National House of Representatives, 1807-11, and afterward, an associate judge of Berks County, Pennsylvania. Numerous descendants in this line rendered important service in civic and religious affairs, an outstanding representative in later times being Dr. Henry Melchior Muhlenberg Richards, of Lebanon, Pennsylvania, author of numerous valuable works dealing with Pennsylvania history.

Frederick Muhlenberg grave at Woodlawn Cemetery, Lancaster, Pennsylvania

William A. Muhlenberg

Henry Augustus Muhlenberg

Frederick Augustus Muhlenberg

John Andrew Schulze

# AFTERWORD

Peter Muhlenberg was best known as the Virginia minister who left the pulpit to become an officer in the American Revolution. The stirring sermon he gave allegedly helped to rally many troops to the cause. The story that he hid his colonel's uniform under his robes while doing so is most assuredly a myth, especially the part about unveiling it in the sanctuary.

Muhlenberg was the grandson of the Pennsylvania-German Indian agent, Conrad Weiser, who helped keep the peace in the early 1700s, before the French and Indian War. During this time, Weiser's daughter Anna Maria met and married a Lutheran clergyman, Henry Melchior Muhlenberg, who was credited with founding Lutheranism in the United States. Henry and Anna Maria had eleven children. Two of them were brothers Peter and Frederick.

Both brothers became ministers, but while Frederick followed less strenuous pursuits in the government, Peter took up the sword and became an officer in the Continental Army. He was a loyal follower of George Washington whom he had met by being a minister in Woodstock, Virginia. Though having little experience, Peter proved himself a capable officer, serving throughout the War, and was wounded during the Battle of Yorktown. As the war ended, he was promoted to Major General for his service. He and his brother both served in the First Congress of the United States, Frederick as the first Speaker of the House.

As time passed, many of the supporting cast of the American Revolution have largely been forgotten. Long a hero of Pennsylvania Germans, Peter Muhlenberg was honored with a prominent statue in front of City Hall in Philadelphia. He and Robert Fulton were the two Pennsylvanians chosen to be honored in Statuary Hall in our nation's Capitol building. Then came World War I and World War II. While this is not stated as the reason for moving the Muhlenberg statue away from City Hall—they were putting in a subway underneath it—over the next decades it was moved away and then into storage—only to reemerge on the grounds of the Philadelphia Art Museum in the 1990s.

The peak of Muhlenberg's popularity was around the time following the centennial in 1876, when Philadelphia was the home of a large German immigrant population, many recently arrived thanks to the help of the German Society of Pennsylvania led by Peter Muhlenberg later in his life. As time went by and these immigrants assimilated, there was no longer the strong German-American presence in City of Brotherly Love. It had dispersed into the suburbs and hinterlands. German-speakers had learned English and many went off to war to fight against their original homeland.

Recent research and restorations in Trappe, Pennsylvania, have led to renewed interest in the Muhlenberg clan. Few extended families have made as many contributions to our nation's founding as the Weiser-Muhlenbergs, in diplomacy, religion, government, and the military. Their's is a story of emigration, carving out a life in the wilderness, making peace with the natives, spreading Christianity, fighting for independence, and establishing the government of our nation.

We are all indebted to the loyal, calm, steadfast leadership of Peter Muhlenberg, one of the key figures of our nation's founding.

—Lawrence Knorr

# REFERENCES

*The Life and Times of Henry Melchior Muhlenberg*, Reverend William J. Mann, D. D.

*The Old Trappe Church*, Reverend Ernest T. Kretschmann, Ph.D.

*Documentary History of the Evangelical Lutheran Ministerium of Pennsylvania.*

*Descendants of Henry Melchior Muhlenberg.*" by Dr. H. M. M. Richards, Pennsylvania German Society's publications, Vol. X, part 3.

*Diary of Henry Melchior Muhlenberg for 1776-7*, Collections of the Historical Society of Pennsylvania, Vol. I.

*Pennsylvania, Colonial and Federal*, edited by Howard Jenkins.

*Pennsylvania, Province and State*, Albert S. Bolles, Ph.D., LL.D.

*Pennsylvania Archives*, First Series—Minutes of the Pennsylvania Supreme Executive Council.

*The Life of Major General Peter Muhlenberg*, Henry A. Muhlenberg, 1849.

"Crisis in the Life of Peter Muhlenberg," Reverend William Germann, D. D., Pennsylvania Magazine of History and Biography, Vol. XXXVII, p. 298, and following numbers.

*The History of Saint Michael's Lutheran Church, Philadelphia*, 1843.

*History of Sussex and Warren Counties, New Jersey*, James P. Snell and others.

*History of Hunterdon and Somerset Counties, New Jersey*, James P. Snell and others.

*Virginia: A History of the People*, John Esten Cooke.

*History of the German Element in Virginia*, Herrmann Schuricht.

*The German Element of the Shenandoah Valley*, Dr. John W. Wayland.

*Journal of the Council of the State of Virginia.*

*Virginia Calendar of State Papers.*

*American Archives*, Fourth Series, Vol. IV.

*History of Georgia*, Charles C. Jones, Jr.

*The Struggle for American Independence*, Sydney George Fisher.

*Records of the Revolutionary War*, W. T. R. Saffell.

"Orderly Book of General Peter Muhlenberg," Pennsylvania Magazine of History and Biography, Vol. XXXIII, p. 257, and following numbers.

*The Valley Forge Orderly Book of General George Weedon.*

"Officers' Opinions on the Plans for Winter Quarters, 1777," Pennsylvania Magazine of History and Biography, Vol. XX, p. 398.

*The History of Valley Forge*, Henry Woodman.

Valley Forge Papers, Ellwood Roberts.

*Benedict Arnold*, Malcolm Decker.

*Life of Frederick William von Steuben*, Friedrich Kapp.

*The Smith Family of Pennsylvania*, J. Bennet Nolan.

*History of Congress*, Vol. I.

*Congressional Register*, Vol. I-III.

*Biographical Directory of the American Congress.*

*The Republican Court*, Rufus W. Griswold.

*History of the German Society of Pennsylvania*, Dr. Oswald Seidensticker.

*Saint John's Lutheran Church, 1806-1906*, Reverend E. E. Sibole.

"Frederick A. Muhlenberg," Dr. Oswald Seidensticker, Pennsylvania Magazine of History and Biography, Vol. XIII, p. 184.

Files of Philadelphia and Norristown newspapers, 1790-1807.

# Index

www.ingramcontent.com/pod-product-compliance
Lightning Source LLC
Chambersburg PA
CBHW031132090426
42738CB00008B/1057